You Can't Teach Hungry

Revised First Edition

John Morgan

**TRIAL
GUIDES**™

Trial Guides, LLC

Interior design by Laura Lind Design
Layout by Melissa Gifford
Cover by Miroslava Sobot
Managing Editor: Travis Kremer
Copyeditor: Melissa Gifford
Proofreader: Melissa Lacock

Printed and bound in the United States of America.
This book is printed on acid-free paper.

Contents

PUBLISHER'S STATEMENT

This book is intended for practicing attorneys. This book does not offer legal advice and does not take the place of consultation with an attorney or other professional with appropriate expertise and experience.

Attorneys are strongly cautioned to evaluate the information, ideas, and opinions set forth in this book in light of their own research, experience, and judgment; to consult applicable rules, regulations, procedures, cases, and statutes (including those issued after the publication date of this book); and to make independent decisions about whether and how to apply such information, ideas, and opinions to a particular case.

Quotations from cases, pleadings, discovery, and other sources are for illustrative purposes only and may not be suitable for use in litigation in any particular case.

Any cases described in this book are composites, and the names and other identifying details of participants, litigants, witnesses, and counsel (other than the author of this book) have been fictionalized except where otherwise expressly stated.

All references to the trademarks of third parties are strictly informational and for purposes of commentary. No sponsorship or endorsement by, or affiliation with, the trademark owners is claimed or implied by the author or publisher of this book.

The author and publisher disclaim any liability or responsibility for loss or damage resulting from the use of this book or the information, ideas, or opinions contained in this book.

DOWNLOADABLE CONTENT

Downloadable content provided to buyers of this book may be printed out, duplicated, and displayed by the buyer in connection with his or her practice of law, including use at trial, but may not be otherwise reproduced, distributed, posted, and/or used in any way without additional permission in writing from Trial Guides.

This book references a budgeting template, fee projection report, and other items available for you to download. These files are intended to provide concrete examples of John Morgan's methods and techniques. To download these files to your computer, smartphone, or tablet, go to the following link:

www.trialguides.com/resources/downloads/you-cant-teach-hungry

FOREWORD

Russ Herman

John Morgan, entrepreneur and trial lawyer's trial lawyer, hungered for success. With a keen intellect and passion for justice, he built this country's premier plaintiffs' trial firm brick by brick. You can't teach hungry. But if you are hungry, you can learn the pathway to individual and law firm success.

In this book, John generously shares his formula for law firm and personal professional advancement and longevity. The Morgan view of law firm development is a keen understanding of two principles:

1. Becoming a successful trial lawyer requires critical self-analysis.

2. Trial lawyers, and trial law firms, should always be in a state of becoming.

John teaches the importance of adapting to change and forecasting the state of our art before it comes into being. For example, constant and organized analysis of technology is absolutely necessary. But at the same time he also reminds us that it is the quality of the people within a firm that determines its success. Are they hungry? Are they passionate? Are they team players?

This book, chapter by chapter, formulates plans for determining individual and firm strengths and weaknesses. John shows you how to critically measure and eliminate your weaknesses, as well as accurately perceive and advance your strengths. He also emphasizes present-day quality and professionalism with an eye to the future. John guides us along the road of acceptable risk with careful evaluation, picking the best cases and mentoring the best lawyers—lawyers who are hungry for success.

Like all great trial lawyers, John has had his share of trials and tribulations. But his ability to separate reality from illusion is what sets him apart. He teaches methods to apprehend the present and plan for the future.

The following are a few illustrative topics from the book and some questions that John answers in clear explanation:

- The sustainable practice requires discipline, order, and common vision.

- Your firm should not be a revolving door. If it is, what are the reasons?

- Don't bring a knife to a gunfight. Or as Shakespeare wrote in *Measure for Measure*, "Do not make a scarecrow of the law and let it keep one shape." Are these two different but parallel concepts?

- Challenge yourself and those around you every day. Don't be afraid of challenges or bullies. How do you handle obstacles?

- Learn how to run your firm with a timeline and a business plan. What is a business plan approach you can implement tomorrow?

- Open new avenues of trial practice. Why?

- Plan definite periodic meetings and require attendance and accountability. Why is this important?

- How do you implement your business plan process?

- Decide on published goals and deadlines.

- Avoid but plan for the Black Swans. What is a Black Swan?

- Don't become a lampshade—be a lamplighter. How do I stay hungry, organized, and focused?

The managing partner of our firm has read and reread *You Can't Teach Hungry* half a dozen times and marked more than thirty-six special paragraphs to review and use.

If you dedicate your professional life and passion to following the injunction to "seek justice, relieve the oppressed, take up the cause of the fatherless, and plead the cause of the widow," read and share John's guide to success: *You Can't Teach Hungry*.

I know of no better colleague, friend, and foxhole partner than John Morgan—read, enjoy, and join with John.

1

Plant Your Tree Today

After being around trial lawyers my entire professional life, I have drawn certain conclusions and generalizations about them as a whole. While these characterizations certainly do not apply to all trial lawyers, it has been my experience that childhood and home life play a huge role in developing a trial lawyer's personality.

I do not think there is any question that, of all the types of attorneys in any legal practice area, personal injury lawyers are the ones with the reputation for being nonconformists. The public at large has always had certain problems with lawyers. They blame lawyers for drumming up work by making laws complicated and difficult for laymen to understand. They portray lawyers as greedy, uncaring, and unsympathetic.

Because of this perception, many lawyers want to be further up the lawyer food chain, and personal injury lawyers have been relegated to the bottom. When critics really want to get under our skin, they call us ambulance chasers rather than personal injury attorneys. I have always been amused by that term and the vivid imagery it creates. It connotes the absurd idea of a lawyer actually

1

following an ambulance to an accident scene and engaging the client on their stretcher. Nonetheless, the personal injury lawyer, or trial lawyer, has a special place in the jurisprudence system.

Most trial lawyers I have met along the way share some general background characteristics. Many were poor or near poor. Alcoholism, drug abuse, out-of-work parents, and unstable home lives seem to be common background themes for many of us. Throughout life, authority and bullies were our hot buttons, and as time progressed, many of us vowed to fight back one day. Most of the background stories I have heard from trial lawyers focus on their humble beginnings—working through college and law school and being the first, or one of the first, in their families to achieve such a high degree of education.

Because our backgrounds did not provide our families or us with access to lawyers, the idea of a contingency fee that allows everyone their own keys to the courthouse is compelling. Many trial lawyers have grown up insecure and vulnerable, and they understand desperation. Most importantly, they understand the concepts of injustice and unfairness. For many of us, our life's work became a way for us to seek justice and fairness and to make sure corporate bullies, insurance companies, and Wall Street crooks don't get to run over the little guy without going through us. We are the little guys all grown up, educated, and fiercely passionate about justice.

My background is not much different from the prototypical trial lawyer's. I grew up in Kentucky with two alcoholic parents. The first part of my life was fairly secure, but then my dad started losing job after job. All the typical things that go along with a living in a paycheck-to-paycheck household went on with us—bill collectors, power outages, phones being disconnected. As I got older, my mother's drinking increased; security was a thing of the past when we finally moved to Florida looking for the promised land.

Once in Florida, my mother couldn't hang on as her drinking progressed, and she moved back to Kentucky. My four siblings and I were left with our dad, who bounced from job to job as his drinking continued. Although a very sweet and nice fellow, he just couldn't hold it together. Later in life, my dad came to work at my law practice and was with me until the day he died.

During my second year of college, my brother Tim was in an accident that rendered him a quadriplegic while he was working as a lifeguard at Walt Disney World. It turned out to be only a workers' compensation case, but Walt Disney World fought him tooth and nail. After watching his lawyer at work, I knew what I wanted to do with the rest of my life. His lawyer was ultimately successful, and Tim was provided for in ways he would have not have been had he not hired the right lawyer. Tim works with me to this day and is a vital cog in our very large machine.

In Kentucky, big oak and maple trees surrounded our home. Three streets over, Henry Clay's estate sat in the middle of our neighborhood with majestic gardens, hundred-year-old trees, and breathtaking grounds. The new tract home we bought when we moved to Florida had two little perfunctory trees in front of the house. The smallness and the plainness of the house was surreal. The stark, ticky-tacky neighborhood was depressing, and the row of houses, each with two seedlings, made a lasting first impression. The memory of all of those majestic trees growing in front of brick houses in Kentucky was replaced with Florida tract homes and two seedlings that probably cost three dollars each.

The reason I bring that memory up is because it is very important to where we begin. Over the course of this book, I am going to make suggestions, tell you about pitfalls I have found in my own practice, make predictions about the future, and, hopefully, give you a road map for you to use in build your own multimillion-dollar law firm. However, as you go to seminars, read books, or have general bull sessions with peers, one of the most depressing things is that years can go by before you have made the necessary changes to build a sustainable and profitable law firm.

For example, I wish I had branded my firm with a vanity phone number early in my career. I didn't until about five years ago. I can only imagine the value of that number had I obtained it twenty-five years ago when I first started my practice. However, as they say, better late than never. As we move forward and you receive new tips and suggestions, I would like you to remember an old adage: **The best time to plant a tree was twenty years ago. The next best time to plant a tree is today.**

Missteps, bad business decisions, and bad partners or personnel are all mistakes of the past. We all dwell on past mistakes and agonize over the what-ifs, but nothing productive comes from that. We must recognize the only way we are going to get from good to great is to plant those new seedlings today.

I go back to Kentucky once a year to see the horse races. I always take a slow drive through my old neighborhood and sometimes sit in front of my old house for ten or fifteen minutes. The big tree I used to climb still stands in the front yard. A gigantic oak tree peeks over the back of the house, and as you drive down Ridgeway Road, the trees lining it are so enormous they create a canopy over the street to Henry Clay's home. It is a comfortable place for me to return to. I often think we are not much different from the salmon that have a desire and need to return to their birthplace.

Despite Kentucky's pull, I must tell you I still live in the same city in Florida we moved to forty years ago. From time to time, I drive through that original neighborhood. Those same seedlings that gave us no shade, comfort, or aesthetic value now tower in every yard up and down that old tract home neighborhood. They are majestic, beautiful, and they provide the only real beauty on that street. The tract homes are still tract homes, just older. Those little, three-dollar seedlings are much more. Those oak trees could sit in front of mansions, courthouses, or any other magnificent structure in the United States. It seems like yesterday we moved from Kentucky to this hotter-than-hell state called Florida, and those seedlings looked like they couldn't take one good, hard, windy rain. Today, those trees that were planted the week we moved in are as sturdy and solid an oak as you will find anywhere.

So as we advance, I hope I will provide you with help, guidance, and suggestions to enhance your practice and better serve your clients. Please don't be discouraged to discover things you should have done yesterday, last year, or even ten years ago. It really doesn't matter. What matters is you identify those areas that need work, make corrections where needed, and implement the suggestions you find valuable as you build your multimillion-dollar law firm.

Remember: The best time to plant a tree was twenty years ago. The next best time to plant a tree is today.

2

THE TORTOISE
AND THE HARE

I remember being introduced to the story of "The Tortoise and the Hare" as a young boy. The story disturbed me because I identified with the Hare. The Hare was fast, clever, and full of confidence. The Tortoise, on the other hand, was everything I could not relate to. He was slow, boring, and very cautious. The fact that he won the race troubled me in a profound way.

However, it was one of those books I kept close to my bedside until I progressed to *The Happy Hollisters*, *The Hardy Boys*, and biographies of sports heroes and United States presidents. I must have read that story and looked at its pictures thousands of times. What always struck me when flipping through the pages was the self-assured look on the Hare's face and the dull look on the Tortoise's. I also remember the other animals that had gathered at the starting line, all confident in the outcome. How could a slow tortoise who was packing a hard, heavy shell even dare to race one of nature's fastest creatures? I remember thinking, "Why would anybody write this story? It has such a predictable ending."

The first time someone read the story to me, I was shocked. When we flipped that page and saw the Hare out of gas and clutching his sides as the Tortoise plodded on, I became upset. The next pages continued to make me anxious, and every time I would turn to a new page, it was my hope and belief the Hare would gather himself and, in the end, pass the Tortoise.

As we all know, that is not how the story ends. Instead, the Tortoise, barely winded and looking incredibly fresh, saunters past the finish line where the entire city of animals stand opened-mouthed in disbelief. That story, as troubling as it was, has remained with me my whole life. As disappointed as I was upon the first reading, I eventually realized the valuable lesson I had been taught. After practicing personal injury law for my entire twenty-five-year legal career, I have seen my share of tortoises, and I have seen my share of hares. I am sure you have seen them in your cities and in your communities. What the strategy of the Tortoise brings to your practice is what my friend and college roommate, Mike Papantonio, has called the *sustainable practice*.

A sustainable practice is one that has predictable income patterns and endures year in and year out. Every so often, it also has spectacular years that prove to be a refreshing jolt. The sustainable practice requires discipline, order, and a group of people who share a common vision. As I have watched new firms forming throughout America over the years, I have found more firms are made up of hares than of tortoises. In the world of lawyers, the trial lawyer is probably the brashest and most confident and can, in some cases, exude an arrogance that is a 100-percent turnoff.

It is usually easy to spot the hares. They are lawyers who have had quick success or a couple of sizeable verdicts early in their careers. Early success can either be the cornerstone and foundation for a future or a recipe for absolute disaster. The problem with early success, especially when it comes out of nowhere, is it can give a lawyer the misconception that this will be his life and law will be as easy in the foreseeable future.

I remember a lawyer in my hometown by the name of Mick O'Brien, may God rest his soul. He left an insurance defense firm when he was in his late twenties because the senior partner was moving to a new venture and decided he did not want to bring Mick along for the ride. Mick was a poor Irishman who had exceeded all of his family's expectations. He had gone to law school and then had been hired by the prestigious law firm Akerman Senterfitt. Mick was devastated by not being included in the move, but he used the slight to his advantage and set out to prove his former employer wrong.

His early days were spectacular. Mick practiced only workers' compensation law at a time when that practice was very lucrative in Florida. His nature and background meant that Mick ingratiated himself with unions and lawyers in the community. He built a big book of business very quickly.

Very early on in his new firm's success, he brought on a partner who had been with him at Akerman Senterfitt named Jim Hooper. Jim was a brilliant lawyer, very eccentric and Mick enjoyed his company. Jim wore a full, Charles Manson-type beard, a ponytail, and a wide variety of glasses. Mick had a shock of prematurely graying hair, bragged about his prowess as a kickboxer, and both Jim and Mick bought front-row, Jack Nicholson style seats at the Amway Center.

Shortly after hiring Jim, Mick represented a dancer who had been paralyzed on the job and told me he received a million-dollar fee for his efforts. Whether it was actually a million dollars or not is questionable. Mick did not mind doubling or tripling numbers. In any event, it was a substantial fee, and the two hares raced off their starting blocks.

Mick and Jim had started their practice at about the same time I started mine in 1985. In fact, we worked on the same floor and were very good friends. With their newfound success, both Jim and Mick seemed to change, becoming bolder, more sure of themselves, and, I am sorry to say, arrogant. I went to a Christmas party that year and met up with Mick. We all had on name tags. I remember Mick walking up to me with a name tag that read "Mick $$$." **Mick Money!** Mick had decided to forgo his last name and walk around the party with a very offensive name tag.

In those early days when my office was across the hall from Mick, I used to worry about what I was doing wrong. I had sublet the office, and they had thrown in the furniture to sweeten the lease. Across the hall, Mick's was decorated in black and white lacquer furniture with an upscale feel. When I left my desk to hang out with Mick, I used to wonder what I needed to do differently. I had my own share of union contacts. I constantly took lawyers out for business development lunches. Cases were rolling in, and I too could ingratiate myself with unions and lawyers.

When Mick and I would drink together during those years, he would sometimes say, "Could you imagine if the two of us ever merged our firms?" There was a part of me that was intrigued by the idea of jump-starting my firm with Mick's. I did personal injury work; he did workers' compensation. I was a conservative, do-it-by-the-book guy; Mick was a caricature. I actually contemplated the idea of merging with Mick. However, there were several things I learned as time passed that made me retreat to the side of the Tortoise and reject the lure of the Hare.

First, I learned Mick was paying almost three times as much rent as I was. I had subleased my space with furniture; Mick had a new lease and big tenant improvements, and he had rolled his furniture into the lease. I also learned that the four annual tickets to Orlando Magic games cost almost as much as my lease for the entire year. Because I was close by, I saw the lack of structure and planning across the hall. Finally, it became clear that workers' compensation would be an area big business would continually attack and chip away at during my legal career.

I vividly remember watching Mick flourish across the hallway. It was during those days I recalled "The Tortoise and the Hare." I told my wife what I believed my business motto for life would be: "Nothing is about today; everything is about tomorrow."

When I say, "Nothing is about today; everything is about tomorrow," I am talking about my business philosophy as it relates to the practice of law. There are many short-term benefits that must be sacrificed for the long-term objective. I have found most hares live for today, for the moment. I have found most tortoises think far into the future. Did you know some tortoises live to be over a hundred years old? Likewise, the lawyer with the short-term approach is flashy, flamboyant, and burns through cash like Freddie Mercury on a binge.

I would like to suggest to you to go out and buy a version of "The Tortoise and the Hare" and leave it somewhere in your office where you will see it every single day. At the end of the day, this childhood story provides a key life lesson for businessmen in general and trial lawyers in particular.

I will be specific about taking the approach of the Tortoise in your business life. I have always been amazed by the lawyers who move into offices that are nicer than their homes early in their careers. They drive leased cars that cost more than their mortgage payments or their rented condominiums. I have long said I would much rather work in a B building and live in an A+ house. There are B and even C+ offices that will get the job done for you. You are much better off using that money for costs on your cases, marketing purposes, and keeping the powder dry for a day that you may need it. Your peers and neighbors will be much more likely to root for you when you are humble, hungry, and working with humility. Arrogance, braggadocio, and just downright obnoxious behavior does not make your peers want to reach out and help you. Finally, it is important to remember our careers last forty, fifty, sometimes sixty years. This race is a long one. It is the most important race you will run in your professional life.

I cannot begin to count all the hares I have seen in my life who now toil miserably for insurance defense firms, work as associates, or, even worse, as "of counsel" in other personal injury firms. Some of these fast-moving hares here in Florida have even had to file personal bankruptcy and take jobs with old competitors.

In one of my favorite books, *The Millionaire Next Door: The Surprising Secrets of America's Wealthy*, two professors take a look at two doctors who make exactly the same amount of money but have very different net worths. I was struck by the idea that, in a household with one working partner, it is important for one spouse to play good offense (to make money) and for the other spouse to play good defense (to run the household on a tight budget). Likewise, to be a profitable tortoise with a sustainable law firm, it's important for the partnership to play good offense and good defense.

In a law firm, playing good offense consists of developing business, trying cases with success, and building a good reputation within the trial community. Playing good defense means running the law firm like a business, being conservative in your spending, and worrying about tomorrow much more than about today. As trial lawyers, we tend to be gregarious risk-takers by nature. It is hard to take on the role of the Tortoise. However, you will find that as life goes on, planning, patience, and purpose can yield spectacular results. The law firm Motley Rice in South Carolina has endured for decades. It has taken chances because it had the resources to do so, and it has flourished over time because the powers that be had a crystal clear vision. As you begin to build your successful trial practice, take this fable to heart. It has worked for countless businesses, for countless professional athletes who turned into champions, and for the best lawyers and law firms in our time. **Remember: Nothing is about today; everything is about tomorrow.**

3

ONLY THE PARANOID SURVIVE

Have a Plan

As I meet with trial firms, socialize with trial lawyers, and give lectures and talks, the most glaring weakness I regularly find is that most firms have no plan—not for the short term nor for the long term. Most firms I meet with just hope that things will always work out. They have no reason as to why; they just hope like hell that they will.

I am also amazed that almost none of these firms conduct their business like a business. Many personal injury law firms across America are unorganized and unstructured. These lawyers are extremely talented and gifted in the art of law but sometimes totally devoid of any business intuition. Even businesses that are less profitable than the trial firm such as painting contractors, heating and air conditioning services, and the usual mom-and-pop businesses, conduct their business with much more sophistication and structure. The typical millionaire next door relies heavily on accountants, business lawyers, and consultants. Yet many law firms rely on none of these.

More shocking, there often are no scheduled partner meetings, planning meetings, or budget meetings. I have found most firms I come into contact with do not even have a budget, much less a budget meeting. How one can operate a business without setting a budget at the beginning of the year and making certain assumptions for fees collected is beyond me.

In short, the typical personal injury law firm in America does not have a plan. It does not have a budget, goals for fees, a business development plan, or meet on a regular or structured basis. As my grandmother would say when looking at a situation that seemed to be thrown together, "It looks like it just happened." For most law firms, this is what goes on year in and year out. It just happens. As a result, there is little certainty and much apprehension as the possibility of building a sustainable law firm gets more and more remote.

As I write this book in the summer of 2009, I cannot begin to tell you of the law firms that have failed this year, are failing, or are on the cusp of failing. The conversations I have had with conferrers throughout America were shocking. They did not have plans, and they did not treat their businesses like businesses. Andy Grove, the great Intel CEO, wrote a book titled *Only the Paranoid Survive*. When I came across that title in the bookstore, I froze. It felt like that book was calling out for me to read it. I did read it, and it is how I have governed my business for the past twenty-five years. Paranoid? Yes. Frightened? Constantly. Worried about failure? I wake up in cold sweats to this day.

For many, the fear of failure is always with us. It is amazing how many great CEOs and entrepreneurs confess to fearing failure and worrying about being exposed as posers even during the height of their successes. That fear of failure is with me every single day. First, I want to tell you it is extremely healthy to have a fear of failure. When your mantra is "Only the paranoid survive," you don't need an alarm clock, you bring work home, and you work on Saturday. Chris Searcy, a great trial lawyer and friend, has built one of America's great law firms. One day I asked Chris,

"Do you require your attorneys to work on Saturday?" Chris replied, "Nothing is mandatory. However, if they don't come in on Saturday, they know not to show up on Sunday."

When the fear of failure leaves you, I suggest you take your chips off the table; go home; invest in tax-exempt bonds, CDs, and treasuries; and call it a day.

There are generally two groups of people when it comes to handling the fear of failure. The first is composed of people who are scared to death their entire business career. They have no plan. They start every year just *hoping* something will work out. And for most of them, there is a day of reckoning when that fear of failure becomes reality. The second group is composed of people who handle their fear of failure by developing a business plan. We develop a business plan even though we run a law firm. Some lawyers discount the fact that a law firm is a business, believing that practicing law is more of an art form. Melvin Belli, The King of Torts, was one such attorney. When he died in San Francisco, this trial lawyer extraordinaire was bankrupt and mired in costs from mass torts he had ventured into without sufficient planning or adequate knowledge.

When I graduated from law school at the University of Florida twenty-six years ago, the thought of treating a law firm like a business was foreign to most practitioners. Today, with multinational firms, mass tort experts, and advertising lawyers, all this is changing.

As we progress, I will ask you to buy into a very simple concept: as you plant your tree today, you will do so with the resolve to develop a business plan for the future. I will suggest business practices that have been very effective for me during these past twenty-five years. Obviously, all firms are different, and some of these ideas may have no relevance. Like you would in a good cafeteria, feel free to take the courses you find nourishing and leave the nonessential food on the table as you meander from chapter to chapter. I will suggest exercises, structures, and tips that have helped me along the way, so you may want to implement some of them in your practice. It is important to remember that fearing failure is healthy. In fact, if you don't fear failure, I can tell you that you certainly will fail. There is nothing more predictable than the numbskull who goes through life oblivious to the landmines, grenades, and sniper fire. Only the paranoid lawyer survives.

I have been in cocktail sessions and seen a great lawyer or two walk by. Often, some of my drinking companions will say, "That guy sure is lucky." Every time I hear someone say this, I am reminded of the great football coach Darrell Royal and his famous quote: "Luck is what happens when preparation meets opportunity."

If you bought this book believing it may be a panacea for success but you have no work ethic, you can stop reading now. I am going to prepare for you a road map to success. This road map works only if you have a work ethic. Some of us believe we are hard workers when, in fact, we aren't. Those people are in a very dangerous position and will ultimately fail. They are much like those who believe they are very competent but are actually incompetent. I consider those people to be the most dangerous in the world. When I think of this type of person, George W. Bush usually comes to my mind.

As I said, for this book to work, you must have a strong work ethic. You either have it, or you don't. It is hard to learn and is usually something that comes early in life. I have found, for example, almost everyone I know who ever worked a paper route was later very successful in life. Many successful trial lawyers owned paper routes.

I believe that those who grew up poor were given a great blessing because that gave them work ethic. Yet many people who have a work ethic end up going nowhere. The reason for this is that they don't have a plan. The most tragic of all figures is the lawyer who works his or her ass off but goes nowhere. They remind me of the hamster on the spinning wheel. That hamster gets up every day, eats, drinks, and gets on the wheel. By the end of the day, he has run miles, burned hundreds of calories, and is totally exhausted. The tragedy is he has done so in the confines of his cage and has gone nowhere. The trial lawyer without a plan is the same.

For those of you who have that work ethic, who have that desire to always do better, and who have that terrible fear of failure that sits in the pit of your stomach 90 percent of the time, let us break out this road map for success and develop a business plan that will begin the process of building your very own multimillion-dollar law firm.

The tree has been planted. The Tortoise is at the starting line. The paranoid are ready to survive. Let us move on.

4

THE GE WAY

It's the People, Stupid

Throughout my career, I have read many books authored by CEOs, founders of significant companies, and management professionals. As we begin to build and formulate a plan for the future, it is my opinion, and I think the opinion of many experts, that there is nothing more important in any organization than the people who work there. Far too often, law firms make the mistake of believing it really does not matter who sits at the reception desk, who heads up human resources, or who runs the bookkeeping department. I find that attorneys do not analyze the impact of an employee who is not their assistant or paralegal. The short story is, people matter in a very profound way.

One of the first exercises I would like for you and your partners to do is a staff assessment. This exercise is quick and enlightening. Make a list of every person who works in your firm. No one should be excluded. List every name on a legal pad and set two columns labeled yes and no. Next, I want you to ask yourself a simple yes or no question. "Knowing everything I know about this employee's competence and productivity, would I hire this person for the position they currently work if they worked for my competition?" Make sure you and your partners complete the exercise separately. Once you all have completed the chart, compare and contrast your answers.

As simple as this drill is, it will give you the first real snapshot into what must be done going forward. When you look at the results, if the predominate number of answers are yes, you are in good shape. However, if more than 10 percent of your answers are no, you have a boat that is taking on water and prohibiting you and your partners from reaching your full potential.

Jack Welch, the CEO of General Electric in the eighties and nineties, was heralded as a genius. We all now know much of GE's success came from its financial services sector that was, in large part, smoke and mirrors. I must confess I am no fan of Welch for reasons concerning his company's environmental record and Welch's own bombastic style. I will say, however, that I have utilized one of his management skills ever since I read Robert Slater's best-selling book, *Jack Welch and the GE Way*.

Every year Welch had his division managers rate their subordinates in groups of A, B, and C. The evaluation went something like this:

1. First, you identify 20 percent of your subordinates as As. An A is someone who must be kept at all cost. An A is a person who would cause great consternation and disruption if they left your law firm. In short, that person's loss would be devastating to you and the firm. We can all think of some of those As immediately. Take a breath, close your eyes, and think of them.

2. Then you identify your Bs. These are the people who make up 70 percent of your workforce. Bs are also divided into two types. In category one, Bs are identified as those with great potential who can and should develop into As, and

that process should begin immediately. The second category consists of those who do not have the potential to be an A but are certainly solid workers who provide a very good service. Sometimes I think of Bs in terms of a sports analogy. They are the pulling guards on the football team; the great defenders in basketball who gets few points, but are able to hold Kobe Bryant down in scoring; the utility infielder who can move from second to short to third giving the starters, also known as As, a much needed rest. The Bs make up the largest percentage of total employees in our firms.

3. Finally, you must identify the Cs. In short, this is the bottom 10 percent of that division. Welch was a fairly brutal CEO, and GE's division managers were required—in fact ordered—to fire all Cs at the end of the year.

I was always bothered by the fact Welch mandated that 10 percent be fired regardless. I often ask myself, what if the bottom 10 percent of your division is not made up of real Cs, and there are some very capable pulling guards in that group? As a result, as I approach the end of the year, I am not as final and unbending in my management shake-ups. Instead, I identify our workers as As, people whose resignation would be devastating; Bs, the same criteria as laid out before; and finally Cs. For me, Cs do not have to make up 10 percent of my staff. Instead, Cs are those people who bring no value to the firm and will be counterproductive if allowed to remain.

Once you have completed both drills, you will have a tangible blueprint of what must be done. I must tell you that firing people has always been extremely personal to me. As I mentioned earlier, I spent most of my childhood watching my father bounce from job to job. The turmoil it causes families can never be overestimated. However, over time, I have come to realize that if certain blighted branches are not pruned judiciously from time to time, the whole rosebush will soon be jeopardized and may never bloom again.

I suggest a very solid and thorough interview and vetting process before hiring anyone. We give personality tests and focus heavily on résumés. It has been my experience that when I find a résumé that shows a person hopping from job to job, if I hire him, he will be hopping soon from me. Don't waste your time. Instead, look at those people who have remained with a company for long periods. You can never underestimate loyalty and the continuity it brings to your firm.

Finally, as you examine your hiring practices and evaluate your staff, you need to evaluate yourself. You must ask yourself what kind of boss you are and what kind of place your firm is to work. There is a very simple method to determine this. Go back as far as your firm has been in existence and get a list of all of your employees by job description (secretaries, receptionists, paralegals, etc.). Calculate the average number of years or, God forbid, months your average employee stays with you. This will be one of the most eye-opening exercises in your planning process.

In my judgment, staff continuity and longevity plays one of the most important roles in a successful law firm and are the cornerstones of a successful practice. I am most proud of the fact that my first receptionist is still with me. My first bookkeeper is the CFO of our Orlando office, and almost every administrative assistant I have ever hired still works within the law firm. I am also extremely gratified and satisfied that I have so many ten-, fifteen-, and twenty-year anniversaries pop up on an annual basis. Being surrounded by As and Bs for twenty-five years has made a huge difference in my practice. When you take a look at your longevity report, it will be a time for real introspection. When people quit, there is sometimes nothing we can do to prevent it. People get bored, people move, people have friction from time to time. When your firm is a revolving door, and a bad longevity report is staring at you, it is time for action.

The reports and exercises I will ask you to do as we continue are extremely important. Remember this: **information is power.** Many people choose not to step on the scale every day for one reason. They don't want to know the truth. They don't want to have a wedge salad with balsamic vinaigrette for lunch. They want a cheeseburger, french fries, and chocolate lava cake. Without the information I suggest you gather, you will someday wake up to an obese and bloated firm.

At the end of the day, if you determine your firm is a revolving door, it will be for one or more of these three reasons:

1. You are cheap. Money is extremely important to all of us. While appreciation and being kept informed of the future of your firm is very important to your employees, a fair wage for a job well done is extremely important.

2. You are a jerk. This is a very hard concept for many of us to come to grips with. Of course it is never my fault. I have been saddled with bad employees. Ingrates. Incompetence. Lazy ne'er-do-wells. And maybe, as time has gone by, three or four wives too! If your longevity report shows short periods of tenure, it is time to take a long, hard look in the mirror and ask the impossible question: Could it actually be me?

3. You are a cheap jerk. I won't spend much time here, because I find that the people I have identified as cheap jerks are constitutionally incapable of helping themselves or their firms. They are cancers inside their firms, and those cancers will ultimately spread to the bone and kill the body. If you have a partner who is this person, it is time for you or them to leave. Metastasized cancer is incurable. Move on.

You now have the tools and the methodology to begin to take stock of your people, their abilities, and your future. You have the ability and the knowledge to, for the first time, see what kind of firm you have built and what kind of continuity you have there. Without these people decisions, everything else in the book means nothing. These people are the hopes, the dreams, and the future of your firm. If you ignore this section, all the other chapters are moot.

I have always found it helpful to remember this: When a person resigns from your law firm, that person is firing you! Have you ever been fired? Do you remember that feeling? It is the worst in the world. Unless a person resigns because of family situations, age, or infirmity, I take resignations very personally. I was fired because I failed to do my job in providing a secure and stimulating workplace. If you get fired enough times, you may want to consider that it might be you.

Remember: it's the people.

5

APOCALYPSE NOW

Trials, trials, trials—it's war out there. As we continue to assess our people, it is time to move from broad strokes to precision cuts. I am going to ask you the most important question in this book. It is a question I asked myself back in 1991. It is a question so personal and so probing you will be very uncomfortable when you hear it. As uncomfortable as this question will be, I have found it necessary to evaluating your firm and your personnel. Hold on to your seats; here comes the question: if you, a family member, or very close friend were injured in a serious accident or were the victims of medical malpractice and you could hire any firm in your area, including yours, would you hire your own law firm?

I would like you to take a few minutes to sit back and let this question percolate. It is very direct. Knowing everything you know about your firm, would you hire yourself to maximize the value of a case that is important to your loved one's future? Or, knowing what you know, would you hire someone else?

That is a difficult question for many of us.

I would like to make a very painful confession. Back in 1991, I asked myself this question for the first time. Remember, this question applies only to cases of magnitude with serious life-threatening injuries that require tremendous financial support. I was doing a good job bouncing around central Florida and trying low-end cases with mixed results, but I honestly did not believe I had the capability, the skills, and, more importantly, the inclination to develop those skills to answer that question with a yes. It was a moment of clarity and one that shaped my firm's future.

If your answer to the question is yes, you are either in very good shape or you are a delusional blowhard. If your answer to the question is no, you must then ask yourself a second question: What am I going to do about it? It would bother me greatly if I knew for a fact that the clients sitting in my lobby had made the wrong choice and would probably receive between 50 and 70 percent of what their cases are worth—or worse! It would be disheartening at best and sinful at worst.

Back in 1991, when I answered no to that question, I was not upset at all. I knew I had other skills that could be very beneficial to my firm. I had a mind for business, brought in many clients, and enjoyed the business of a law firm. However, I knew that to develop the firm as I envisioned it, I would need to surround myself with warriors, also known as the American trial lawyers. In my mind, there is nothing more gallant than the great trial lawyer who takes his sword and shield throughout America's courtrooms and brings justice to those who do not have the means to take on corporate giants and bullies. There is no more rewarding profession. With all the government regulation and law, no group of professionals brings more safety to Americans than trial lawyers. Whether it's flammable pajamas, tires that split, unsafe pharmaceuticals and medical devices, or unscrupulous insurance companies, the trial lawyer is the great equalizer. When I think of the men and women who are the great ones, I do so with sincere fondness and admiration. On the other hand, I have seen firms that simply take the last best offer, firms that are in it for themselves and have no conscience or desire to help others. They hurt our public perception, and, more importantly, our presuit case values. Because there are attorneys who take the last best offer and refuse to pick up their swords and shields, all of our clients are penalized in the presuit arena.

When I answered no, I set out to surround myself with gladiators: red-meat eaters who thrive in the courtroom and love the smell of napalm in the morning. They are my kind of lawyer and make up my kind of firm.

The next thing that must be assessed as we go forward is the ability and capability of our firm and our lawyers. Are we trial lawyers or are we claim adjusters with a law degree? Are we fighting this battle with bullets or blanks? These are all essential questions. Insurance companies and big corporations are surrounded by bean counters and actuaries who punch and repunch numbers all day long. More importantly, they **know** which firms are fighting with bullets and which firms are fighting with blanks. They know which firms go to trial on a regular basis and which firms haven't seen the inside of a courtroom since Christ was a baby. Insurance companies are bullies, and insurance defense lawyers often take on that personality.

When I was a young boy in Lexington, Kentucky, every Sunday, Tom, the town bully, would visit his grandmother, who lived near my house. And every Sunday he decided one of his Sunday activities would be to beat me up. When he would see me, he would stomp his feet and come charging like a mad bull. But because of my speed, I would run into the house and remain there until his family left his grandmother's home. It made for some very long Sunday afternoons and some very boring days in my backyard.

One snowy day, as Tom charged me in the freezing cold, I stood my ground. My gloves were hard and wet and cold. I hit Tom squarely in the nose, and blood went everywhere. I wish I could say that Tom turned tail and ran, but the blood seemed to fire him up, and he ended up giving me a pretty good ass-kicking. However, that turned out to be the last day Tom ever bothered me, and we became quasi-friends (I never trust bullies). I reclaimed my Sunday afternoons.

The moral of the story is that bullies hate pain. They hate tasting their own blood. And at the end of the day, they are actually cowards. If you believe insurance companies don't know who you are, your reputation, and the likelihood you will actually go to trial, think again. Bullies always pick on those who run. I want to repeat this with emphasis. **Bullies always pick on those who run.**[1]

Have you noticed that every time the United States of America has gone to war since Vietnam, we have picked targets that are much like the inept claims adjusters and lawyers? When there was unrest in Tiananmen Square in China, as offended as we were, we did nothing. When the Soviet Union moved into Georgia and committed atrocities, as offended as we were, we did nothing. When Kim Jong-un, the leader of North Korea, deployed missiles and built nuclear devices, we did nothing.

No, we left China, Russia, and North Korea alone. Instead, our battles have been less than epic. Ronald Reagan was forced to invade the global threat Grenada! The insurgents had taken over St. George's Medical College, and we deployed rangers, paratroopers, Navy SEALs, and the elite of the elite to quell the unrest. When Saddam Hussein, a certified madman with no weapons of mass destruction, decided to invade Kuwait, we were there. The Persian Gulf War took only a few days, and I believe the final Iraqi soldiers surrendered to Sam Donaldson somewhere in the desert. Finally, when the second George Bush decided to invade Iraq, it only took a few weeks. Mission accomplished!

The next exercise examines the number of trials your firm has had in the last five years. I say five years because I am tired of going to lunches and hearing old lawyers talk about that big

---

1. As a side note, on top of being an effective trial lawyer, it helps to be crazy. Ted Babbitt of West Palm Beach, one of America's great trial lawyers and a member of the Inner Circle, once told me, "I'm like a pit bull. Once I hook onto your leg, I am going to rip it off or you are going to kick my head in."

verdict they got in 1976. This is an exercise I undertook five years ago with alarming results.

Have every lawyer in your firm put together two lists. The first is a list of all their settled cases and the settlement amounts. To the right of each case, have them note whether it settled in presuit, for policy limits, in suit, or during trial. This can be cumbersome, but it can also be extremely enlightening. Remember, information is power.

Next, have each lawyer, you included (assuming you have an active practice), list all their trials with the venue, date, verdict, last offer before verdict, and name of the carrier. What you will see is what the insurance companies already know—whether you are fighting with bullets or blanks. On one side, see the number of cases your lawyers have settled, and on the other side, see the number of cases that have actually gone to trial and verdict. It should be done in writing because nothing is as stark or impactful as numbers in black and white.

When I did this exercise, I found that I had lawyers in my firm who had not been to trial—not once—in five years. I found I had lawyers in my organization who were simply taking the last best offer. Upon seeing this in black and white, I found that I had failed many of my clients by allowing these lawyers to get away with what I would describe as legal malpractice.

There are several reasons lawyers don't go to trial:

1. They are lazy. If this is the case, you will have answered this question back when you were doing your As, Bs, and Cs and asking yourself if you would hire an employee if he worked for your competition. This trial report may simply be the icing on the cake.

2. They are scared. This also should have come out in your employee evaluation. A scared trial lawyer is like a scared matador.

3. They don't know how. Now, this one may surprise you, but it has been my experience that there are many, many so-called

trial lawyers—and I use that term loosely—who cannot try a case first chair. They have come to your firm after hiding in insurance defense firms and taking depositions for years. Or they have come to your firm and have done a good job of hiding, bobbing, and weaving. The truth is, they cannot try a case first chair, and you don't know it or have chosen to ignore it. We can ignore it no longer. This is war.

I repeat: **this is war**! After you examine your presuit settlement report and compare it to your trial report, you will know what kind of warriors you have in your firm. You will also know what kind of action you **must** take.

Years ago, when I first completed this survey, I was shell-shocked. I found that I had lawyers who had not tried a single case in at least five years and who undoubtedly were simply taking the last best offer. I understood that I had some lawyers who were lazy, scared, incompetent, or a combination thereof, and I had been able to weed out certain lawyers through twenty-some odd years of ABC tests, but this trial test opened my eyes like never before. I discovered lawyers who were not warriors at all, and I was able to implement a plan that gave them the opportunity to be warriors or to turn in their swords and shields. I convened a meeting in our Orlando office and announced that going forward, every lawyer in the firm would be required to try **at least three first-chair jury trials a year**. All change is met with scoffs and howls, but this suggestion was met with outright indignation from some. As a consequence for not trying three jury trials a year, each non-complying lawyer would forfeit twenty-five thousand dollars of their compensation.

Some of the lawyers protested that this was an ethical viola-tion, that I was forcing them to try cases that should not be tried. I assured them of two things. One, that they would find there were plenty of cases to be tried and finding three would not be difficult; and two, that the real ethical violation was the past five years (and in some cases longer) in which certain lawyers had only accepted final offers from insurance companies. It is impossible that the insurance companies had paid them **fairly** in each and every one of their cases. We know, as trial lawyers, that insurance companies are not run by fair people. They are businesses. Their business is to take in premiums and pay out as little as possible. Our job is to ensure our clients get justice.

When a lawyer meanders through life in the firm, not trying a lawsuit for years and years at a time, you have a C in your midst—a cancer that is affecting the entire reputation of the firm. And, in the end, enough of these folks will kill the firm.

I am pleased to report that the implementation of this three-trials rule has been extremely successful. We have won over 80 percent of our jury trials. Our lawyers believe in themselves and know juries will do the right thing. Our clients have benefited by receiving these verdicts. Most importantly, however, is that now that the insurance industry knows we are not only a firm that will take cases to trial, but also a firm that is required to take cases to trial, our reputation has grown exponentially.

One tree you should plant today: insist upon being a trial lawyer firm—not a personal injury firm. There is a difference, my friends. You will find that should you implement this plan after your review, the troops will be invigorated, your support staff will be proud of who they work for, and your clients will receive the justice they are entitled to.

Do not kid yourself in believing that somehow the insurance industry does not know who we all are. In Los Angeles, California, I can assure you the insurance industry knows who Brian Panish is. They know that when they draw that name, they have drawn a natural born killer. They know that a case in the hands of Brian Panish is worth five to ten times the value of a case in the hands of a lesser lawyer. They know who we are. They know who you are. Reputation means everything, and it is in your control.

Don't bring a knife to a gunfight.

6

You Can't Send a Duck to Eagle School

The Greatest Show on Earth

In the previous two chapters, I gave you tools to evaluate the people in your firm, the talents they possess, and the results they are receiving. This is fairly straightforward.

However, because having the right people do the right things is so important—in fact, it is 95 percent of the essence of this book—I must spend one more chapter clarifying certain conceptions and misconceptions. The reason I say 95 percent is because without the proper people to implement and follow this map, everything I say will be of little or no value.

One of the most common mistakes I see in every business is the tendency of the managers and partners to hire people who do not threaten or challenge them. This is the start of a slippery slope to decline. In big corporations, what often happens is that As hire Bs, the Bs hire Cs, and Cs hire who knows who. This takes place because most managers do not like feeling threatened. They do not like being challenged. As a consequence, before long, their organization is infested with mediocre and worse-than-mediocre personnel.

Let me explain it in terms we all understood as children. Most of us have been to a circus at one time or another. When I mention the term circus, all of us have certain preconceived notions of what will be under that big top. Imagine how you would feel if you went to the circus with your family and friends, and when you got inside, you found a much different circus than you had expected. What if the circus animals consisted of seals, otters, a few squirrels, and some ponies? What if the circus had a few older clowns running up and down the aisle? What if this circus trotted out three or four broken-down elephants holding each other's tails and circling the arena as its grand finale? Your disappointment would be palpable. Had you known about this circus, you never would have gone in the first place. And you know full well that circus is doomed to fail because it has put together The Most Miserable Show on Earth.

Building a law firm is much like building a circus. As I have put together my legal circus, I have been very aware of what the public expects and wants. As you begin to build your law firm, think of it as building The Greatest Show on Earth.

What do people really want to see when they go to the circus? They want to see the great Wallenda walking on a high-wire, almost touching the top of the tent, with no net below. They want to see this because, subconsciously, they have come to see him fall. They want to see the animal trainer walk into a cage filled with lions and tigers growling, slashing, and roaring at the top of their lungs. They have paid their money, bought their cotton candy, and nestled into their seats with their family hoping to see the man eaten alive. And finally, at the end of the circus, the human cannonball is loaded into a gigantic gun, packed with gunpowder, and blown out across the arena. The fans sit there hoping he misses the net and is blown into Helena, Montana.

When you begin to build The Greatest Show on Earth, it is important you understand that without taking risk and without risking your very existence every single day, you have nothing more than a two-dollar petting zoo filled with manure and horseflies. When you build The Greatest Law Firm on Earth, you must surround yourself with tenacious litigators, bright thinkers, and warriors who will demand much of you emotionally and financially. For many of you, this demand may be too much.

You will find yourself constantly worrying that these lawyers will leave with cases and other law personnel. You will find yourself fretting about their demands for money. Being surrounded by these human lions will frighten you, bringing out your own insecurities, because you may not believe in yourself or believe in the importance of having a law firm that you don't just make a living in, but that you are proud of.

The lions can eat the trainer anytime they want, but they don't because they are well fed. Nick Wallenda can fall off that high wire at any given day, but wire-walkers usually don't fall because they are practiced, focused, sober, and disciplined. The human cannonball has scientifically figured his routine out, knows just the right amount of gunpowder to load, and points the barrel in exactly the right direction; a safe landing occurs in every single show.

If you don't have the courage to surround yourself with the best and brightest (and perhaps the most egotistical), you may well have a very nice firm and make a very fine living. But you will never have what you sometimes dream about, and you will always wonder why you didn't pull the trigger.

One of the key ingredients I look for in my lawyers is something you may never have thought of before, something that only exists in a small part of the population. There are two types of lawyers in the personal injury world. There is the lawyer with the satiable appetite and the lawyer with the insatiable appetite. It is very difficult during interviews or psychological tests to determine which lawyer will have the insatiable appetite. However, your goal should be—and mine is—to find that lawyer who has an insatiable appetite.

What do I mean by an insatiable appetite? If a person makes $250,000 this year but will not be satisfied if he makes the same amount next year, he has an insatiable appetite. If he makes $1 million dollars this year, he will be very dissatisfied if he makes anything less than that next year. They are the trial lawyers whose successes this year will mean nothing when next year begins. Those old trials from last year will be a distant memory, and only fresh kills will satisfy their egos and desire to win.

Unfortunately, these men and women are very few and far between. Most trial lawyers have what I have described as a satiable appetite. In other words, they think, "If I could make $250,000 a year for the rest of my life, I'd be okay." Or, "If I can have a verdict every two or three years, that's fine by me. I enjoy my weekends." These satiable critters are extremely annoying because, they regale you with stories from their one trial five years ago while you are having drinks with them at happy hour. And by the way, they've talked about the same trial at every single happy hour you can remember. When a firm takes on these satiable lawyers, the hunger in the firm and the desire for championship begins to wane, and the firm soon begins to die.

Finding a lawyer with an insatiable appetite is really not too difficult. As one famous Supreme Court opinion stated when discussing pornography, "I know it when I see it." If I asked you to identify the members of your firm with satiable appetites and those with insatiable appetites, your answers would undoubtedly match your partners'. We know who these people are. More importantly, we know who these people aren't, yet inexplicably do nothing about it.

I will give you one test that will help you. It is not foolproof, but I have found it pretty darn close to foolproof. On a weekend or at night after nine o'clock, email a question to your lawyers. You will find that the killers, those with insatiable appetites, will respond within the hour. You will find that in many cases, a message sent out on Friday night may not be returned until Monday morning when the satiable slug returns from a weekend of leisure.

Money never sleeps. And neither does the lawyer with the insatiable appetite.

Remembering the happy hours I have endured with C lawyers talking about that *one* trial that took place over fifteen years ago, I am reminded of something one of America's greatest product liability lawyers, John Overchuck, asked me. "Have you ever noticed no one ever talks about the great settlements they have received in their lives? They only talk about the trials." It is so true, and there is an important lesson to be learned in that statement.

The reason the blowhard at happy hour continues to tell us about that big case he tried in 1976 is because **he knows he should have been doing that in 2009.** He knows trying cases is what he is hired to do and is supposed to do. He tells this one story over and over again as if it will somehow disguise the ruse he has been maintaining for the last twenty years. He is ashamed of himself, and that is why he doesn't order a round of beers and brag about the settlements he has knocked down this fiscal year. There is real shame in calling yourself a trial lawyer or calling your firm a trial firm and then realizing you are nothing but a group of posers pretending you are something you are not. Remember this: everyone knows who you are and what you are.

Before I close this chapter, I want to leave you with a very important lesson. One of the things we do as human beings is try to change peoples' conduct or behavior. We try to make people something they have no chance of being at all.

You can't send a duck to eagle school. Even if you send a duck to eagle school and the mama eagle teaches that baby duck everything she knows, no matter what, that duck will never be able to do what an eagle does. The duck simply does not have the wingspan, the beak, or the talons necessary to be an eagle. It just won't happen.

There are people who are not funny. If you take an unfunny person and sequester them in a room with Ellen DeGeneres, Chris Rock, and Don Rickles for thirty days and then have them stand on a stage to do a comedy show, I promise you they will bomb.

You either have it or you don't have it. It is as simple as that. For those of you who have a lawyer in your office that you are trying to develop, stop wasting your time. It is never going to happen. When I coached my children's baseball teams and we had tryouts, it didn't take me long to see which boys would be the stars and which boys would struggle. All I needed to do was hit the boy a couple of balls to shortstop, watch him throw the ball, and then watch him run in to take a swing with the bat. All I needed was one or two pitches, and I could tell within a real degree of baseball certainty whether I had an A, a B, a C, or someone who should never have been at tryouts in the first place.

These lawyers in your office are in Little League tryouts right now. You have hit the two ground balls to shortstop; they have taken their swings. You know what you have. So what are you going to do with this information? Remember, information is power. There may be many reasons you choose not to take action. He may be your son. Worse, he may be your sister's son. Whatever the reason, I would choose to take the action that is needed. Please know this inaction is costing your firm success, is turning your circus into a pony ride, and is moving your firm closer to a bad end.

These last three chapters have given you all the tools you need to do what you must. The only question now is: do you have the will to do so? Past behavior is the best indicator of future behavior. Leopards do not change their spots, and the older a leopard is, the more certain you must be that those spots are there forever.

Several years ago, Jeremy Foley, athletic director at the University of Florida, fired head coach Ron Zook midseason. Many people didn't understand why he would do so. Foley replied, "You need to do today what you are going to have to do in the future. Why wait?" That is the question for you as you continue reading. Why wait?

Happy flying. Remember that eagles don't flock; they gather one at a time.

7

RICH DAD—POOR DAD[2]

Your Own Stock Market

During the stock market bubble, I was amazed and dismayed at the time and attention American businesspeople spent poring over quotes from the stock market. People had CNBC blaring in their offices all day long as they watched the stock market fluctuate. Water cooler chatter was annoying, to say the least.

We couldn't get enough of magazines like *SmartMoney*, *Fortune*, and *Forbes*. The *Kiplinger Letter* and the *Wall Street Journal* were must-reads. Like zombies in a hypnotic trance, men and women throughout America were mesmerized by Wall Street and all the crooks who we now know were simply manipulating irrational exuberance. Many times, these same people who devoted their attention to studying the stock market and the so-called masters

2. Robert T. Kiyosaki, *Rich Dad Poor Dad: What the Rich Teach Their Kids About Money—That the Poor and Middle Class Do Not!* (Plata Publishing 2011).

of the universe had little or no money in the market, yet everyone became an expert. Day trading flourished.

While other people were hunched over their corned beef hashes and scanning yesterday's market results with a magnifying glasses, I used to ask myself, "Are they paying as much attention to their own **businesses** as they are to these businesses that are being manipulated by high tech crooks?" While Bernie Madoff and Allen Stanford were churning out 12-percent returns on a yearly basis, these robots were easily digesting all of this information on a twenty-four hour basis and ignoring what was going on inside their own shops.

I hope we have learned our lesson, but history suggests we haven't. Just think of the tulip mania that hit Holland hundreds of years ago. Greed motivates us in irrational ways. Now, as we catch our breath after watching our 401(k)s plummet and all of these titans being hauled off to jail, it is time for us to begin the process of monitoring our own stock market.

It is my firm belief that a capable person will never make more money—stock market included—than by investing in himself. For most of you, I predict the single best investment you have ever made is in yourself. Consequently, as you begin to refocus and plant new trees, it is important you have information on a yearly basis that shows you how your own personal stock market is doing. That stock market is **you**!

My suggestion is two-prong. First, gather your income tax return for the past seven years. If you have been practicing for less time, use whatever years are applicable. Go through those years and write them down on a piece of paper. After you have finished compiling the information, take a piece of graph paper and build your own personal stock market.

Plot the years of your income and the related amounts on this graph. When you do this, you will be looking at just the very charts you might have pored over at the local Denny's two years ago. However, instead of dissecting the graph of Cisco's earnings for the past seven years, you will be taking a look into the mirror, the mirror of your own personal stock market.

Once you have done this, you will have the first visual of your professional life. It is like stepping on a scale. For some of you, this graph will be encouraging, and for others, it will be just the opposite. Regardless of how you feel, you will have information that will enable you to begin the planning process for the first time. As painful as this exercise is, it must be done on a yearly basis.

The second thing I want you to do is complete the same exercise with total fees and net profits for your firm. This exercise will give you three graphs that will provide you a stunning visual snapshot into the business of you.

You may find that while your fees have increased, your net profit and personal income have decreased. You may find that during the last seven years, your fees, net income, and personal income have gradually sloped upward. Unfortunately, some will find just the opposite. For others still, an alarming pattern may appear. That is a pattern of peaks and deep, deep valleys. For your purposes of building your practice, what the charts demonstrate doesn't matter as much as what you plan to do with this very vital information.

When you complete this exercise, you will have an accurate visual reading of your own personal stock market. It will show you how **your company** is doing. It will tell you more than I could ever tell you in this whole book. The information you glean from this drill will be a wake-up call in some cases, and, in others, it will be an affirmation that what you have been doing all along is valid and that your plan and execution have worked. In either event, the exercise is a vital one.

I've said this before and will say it many times: **information is power**.

8

Systems from Good to Great[3]

Through my entire legal career, my practice has been limited to plaintiffs' personal injury work. I decided to write this book to impart my failures and my accomplishments, but, most importantly, to pass on to you the things I have learned—sometimes the hard way. This is a book about lawyering and about business.

To reiterate, it has been my observation that some of the greatest lawyers in this country are terrible businesspeople. *It has also been my observation that most lawyers don't run their practice like a business.* Instead, most law firms throughout America haphazardly go through the motions without a plan, without structure, and with no order. The first thing I would like to suggest to you is that you run your business and your law firm exactly the way a bank or insurance company would run their company.

---

3. Jim Collins, *Good to Great: Why Some Companies Make the Leap... and Others Don't* (Harper Business: 2001).

There is no doubt that you have made business investments during your life—stocks, bonds, private placement offerings. Some of those investments have paid off and some probably have not. *However, I would suggest to you again that the greatest single investment you will make in your lifetime is in yourself.* The greatest return you will receive in this world will most likely be from your law firm. With that said, the question becomes: Why do I not run my business the same way I would expect the other investment vehicles I have purchased through the years to be run?

I would like to suggest some early steps in running your business like a business. The first thing is to establish a budget for your firm. Every successful company has a budget. That is your benchmark for what you need to do, at a minimum, to make a profit. In the downloadable content for this book,[4] you will find a template that I use at my firm in Florida. This template is a guide for you and only a guide. There may be many expenses and items that are part of your firm that are not a part of mine. The first step is simple, though: put a budget together and follow that budget through the year. The second thing I do every year is put together my fee projections for the upcoming year. I survey my lawyers and get a rough estimate of what they plan to do in fees. I also use historical fees as a benchmark By having fee projections and a budget, you will be—maybe for the first time—prepared to begin your new year of running your business like a business.

I cannot over emphasize the importance of these two tools. Each month, a budget report showing you exactly what your expenses are and how they vary from your budget must be forwarded to your desk. At the same time, your fee projection report should be forwarded to you as well. These two tools will be your monthly barometer for how well you are doing or how poorly the firm may be performing. In any event, you will have information you have

---

4. Downloadable materials such as the budgeting and fee projection templates for *You Can't Teach Hungry* are available at www.trialguides.com/resources/downloads/you-cant-teach-hungry

never had before. *Remember, information is power!* Information is sometimes unfriendly and sometimes unwelcome, but is always necessary. Without these financial information tools, you are simply running your business in the dark. There is no compass. There is no light. There is no direction. These two tools will set you on the path of running an effective law firm.

Once you have made the commitment to implement a budget and fee projection, I would like to suggest a schedule of events that should take place in your firm every single year. These necessary meetings should be calendared and followed rigidly. These meetings and events are no different than those that Fortune 500 companies or the small insurance company down the street have.

Firm Kickoff Breakfast

Every year for almost fifteen years, I have had a firm kickoff breakfast. Today, Morgan & Morgan has more than 1,600 employees in Florida alone. However, we had these kickoff breakfasts when the firm had fewer than ten people. They are important and vital to your firm.

At the kickoff breakfast, you accomplish several things:

1. You acknowledge and publicly recognize team members who have performed well in the past year. Public recognition amongst our peers is extremely important. You can never underestimate the power of public recognition and the power of publicly thanking employees who have made you successful.

2. You provide the firm—and the firm includes everyone—information about the firm: where we are and where we are going. Employees are as interested in being informed as they are in their paychecks. An informed employee is a happy employee. They feel included, in the know, and a part of the team.

3. Finally, you explain the firm's mission and purpose. It is often important to let the entire firm know what it is we

are here to do and accomplish. As plaintiffs' attorneys, our employees can sometimes become callous and forget that our clients come to us in their most desperate times. They may be facing foreclosure on their homes; they may be having trouble paying their bills, and they are all worried about their families. It is important to remind everyone that we work for our clients, and it is we who are the employees and our clients who are the employers. Our clients may not pay us on an hourly fee, but they do pay us a very healthy wage. We need to remind everyone that we should treat our clients the same way we would treat the bank president down the street if she were our client. Our clients deserve this treatment.

The firm breakfast sets the tone for the year and recognizes firm members. Most importantly, it restates and emphasizes our mission statement. We are the key to the courthouse for those who would have no access without us. For some, we are the only thing separating desperation from hope. Finally, we are the civil police that monitors and modifies bad corporate behavior by manufacturers, insurance companies, and other corporate types. You must emphasize that the work of the trial lawyer is important to society and that the work we do is good and noble. You must also emphasize that in working at your firm, your employees are making a significant difference in people's lives. The firm breakfast should occur during the first week in January.

Best Practices Meeting

Shortly after the firm breakfast, you should have a best practices meeting. Depending on the size of your firm, this meeting can include your entire firm or be divided into practice areas. At our firm, it is usually broken up by practice area—medical malpractice, personal injury, workers' compensation, and other practice areas.

The purpose of the best practices meeting is to make sure everyone in the firm is doing things in the most efficient and productive way. We find every year that different people, even though they may be sitting offices apart, are doing things in totally different ways. During this session, we move through our practice areas from the first time a client calls in, to our meetings with them, to the closing statement. This is a long day, but it is most productive. During this meeting, we begin by having lawyers speak substantively about key legal issues that face us every single day. Here are few of the topics we discuss:

- Medicare and Medicaid liens

- Hospital liens

- Bad faith

- Sovereign immunity issues

- Products liability cases within third party and workers' compensation cases

- First party issues

- Litigation pitfalls, especially in the pleading part of the case

These are only suggestions, but we focus on topics that provide pitfalls to all of our lawyers through the year. We address these issues so that our whole team has the best information and the best practices going forward.

During the second half of the afternoon, we spend time going through our forms. As with any practice over the years, form letters are altered and edited, and some form letters are better than others. During this afternoon session, we go through our forms to see if we are all on the same page or if people are doing things differently. Once we determine which forms and procedures are best, we incorporate them across the firm.

Finally, at the end of the day, we open the floor and talk about issues that team members believe have been problematic for us the previous year. Legal secretaries, paralegals and lawyers are all invited. This last hour of the session is usually more informative than you may ever believe. It is at this time that administrative assistants and paralegals tell you things you may have never heard before. You will learn more about your firm by allowing the staff to have this forum than you have learned in all of the last year combined. This is a long but necessary day. This is a day that sets procedures in motion. This is a day that makes your firm a better firm because best practices are implemented as you move forward.

Case Evaluation

Every other Wednesday, we evaluate cases in our firm. I believe lawyers make a terrible mistake by sitting cloistered in their offices, alone and unaided in determining what a case is worth. Case evaluation occurs come hell or high water. During this meeting, lawyers bring in cases for evaluation. They present liability and damages in the light most favorable to the plaintiff—exactly the way they would present them in a demand letter. After that, firm members can ask questions. These are the same questions an attorney would face from the insurance adjuster or from the defense attorney. This session prepares you for what lies ahead by forcing you to explain to your colleagues how you plan to prove your case.

You will find that this mandatory case evaluation meeting will provide you with great results. It forces lawyers to think about what lies ahead and to be prepared instead of just winging the same old demand letter. In the early years, if someone was evaluating a slip-and-fall case, there would be questions like, "Where is the picture of the floor? How long was the substance on the floor? How can you prove that?" By forcing lawyers to be prepared at the case evaluation meeting, you will do your clients a great service. If you force a lawyer to have a meeting with his peers, he will be more prepared than if he is operating on his own in an office with no scrutiny or peer pressure. This case evaluation results in better lawyering, better client satisfaction, and better results. It will lay the foundation for better preparation should this case go to trial. This meeting is never canceled at my firm. It is absolutely mandatory.

Partner Meeting

When I ask people around the country how often they have partner meetings, I can't tell you how many times I get statements like this:

- "From time to time we talk about issues at lunch."

- "If we have a problem, we walk down to each others office."

- "We never have partner meetings."

Would you invest money in a business where the CEO, CFO, and key members didn't have regular meetings? Would you invest in any Fortune 500 company that operated their business without some accountability and planning? I don't think so.

I recommend you hold partner meetings once a month. Our partner meetings are held on the first Monday of each month at 3:30 p.m. Attendance is mandatory. It is important that assistants understand not to set mediations, depositions, or client meetings during that time. The only excuse for missing a partner meeting is trial, death, or preplanned vacations. You will find that by having the structure of these meetings, problems don't accumulate and business runs smoothly. Make sure all partner meetings have an agenda that is circulated the week before so others may add items. These regular partner meetings will help you run an effective law firm and to begin to develop the habits of highly effective people.

Midyear Planning Session

During our years of practice, we have found it very helpful to have a midyear planning session that takes place in July. Even the best plans that began a year earlier often come off the tracks as the year progresses. During our midyear planning session, we use this time to assess the firm at the halfway point, make adjustments to earlier plans, and begin to formulate our plans for the following year. By taking the time to meet at midyear, you will do your firm and yourself a tremendous favor. At the halfway point of the year, you will be able to see if your budget is on or off target and whether your fee projections meet your expectations. During this meeting, you can primarily assess those two items and also discuss events and occurrences that have developed throughout the year.

This midyear meeting is much less formal and structured than other meetings. This is a time to see if goals are being met, to see if key personnel are keeping up their end, and to talk about problems and trends that may be developing.

It is always important to have this type of meeting outside of your office. I have found throughout the years that when you have these meetings in the office, disruptions abound—phone calls, people and clients dropping in, and other diversions that are not productive.

It is important all decision-makers are at this midyear meeting. As with all scheduled meetings, it can **never** be acceptable practice to have one decision-maker absent. A Fortune 500 company would never tolerate it and neither should you. There will be times when people will make excuses or look for a reason not to attend. The day you allow that to happen begins your slippery slope to returning to an unstructured law firm.

Pre-Budget Meeting

The pre-budget meeting is exactly like it sounds. This is a meeting that can be fairly brief and to the point but essential for the ultimate budget meeting that will be held in November. During this meeting, all key personnel with access to budgetary numbers gather and you delegate responsibilities to ascertain budgetary numbers for the next fiscal year.

For example, it may be the role of administrative personnel, individual partners, an administrative assistant, or limited staff to ferret out these numbers, depending on the size of the law firm. As part of the downloadable content,[5] there is a template that will give you a road map to putting together your firm's budget. During this planning session, you will delegate responsibilities for these

---

5. See www.trialguides.com/resources/downloads/you-cant-teach-hungry

numbers. For example, in the case of a three-person firm, someone would be responsible for the rent or mortgage payments for the following year, someone would be responsible for payrolls and salary, someone would be responsible for office expenses, and so on.

By having this pre-budget meeting, the final budget meeting will be much smoother and much more productive. During your first year of putting your budget together, this meeting will be a learning experience. There may be many misses and miscalculations. However, you will find that as you go forward, this budget will become more exact and very helpful in running a successful law firm. The template I have provided is simply a road map. You may well have other expenses that are not on the template, and they should be added.

A Week to Think

This step is completely optional, but it is one I adhere to on a yearly basis. Some time ago, I read that Bill Gates takes one week out of the year to go off and think. Now I know that seems like a long time, and you must be wondering what you would think about.

You will be amazed and astounded at the productivity that comes from this week. A week does not need to be a total of seven days. It may be Monday through Thursday. No matter how much time you spend alone thinking, you will be rejuvenated to begin the process of building your multimillion-dollar law firm.

The week I spend to think is divided between many different areas. Throughout each year, I have a folder titled "Ideas." Every time I read an article, have a thought, or see something that can benefit my law firm, I place it in this file. It may be an article that I read in the *New York Times* or an idea that I had for the physical plant. No idea is too small for this file.

I also take reading materials that I believe that can be very helpful in the management of my law firm with me. During this week alone, I do a voracious amount of reading and delve into my idea file.

To say that this week is cathartic is an understatement. It begins the process of planning for our next calendar year, and it is a time of reflection planning from which some of my biggest ideas have sprouted. I take the week at my beach house. Long walks alone in the morning are par for the course. During these walks, I spend time going over things I thought about the day before. The endorphins move, the mind is alert, and this brisk walk sets the stage for my day of thinking and planning. During this week, I avoid as many calls as I can and avoid my cell phone if at all possible. I take my meals alone. Solitude and thought is first and foremost.

I can tell you from experience that this week alone is as productive as anything I do all year. It is not enough just to go off on this week without a plan or objectives. You must go with the single purpose of thinking and dreaming. Thinking of ways to make your firm better. Dreaming of ways to make your firm the most successful firm in your community.

As I mentioned, this is an optional week. It is optional for you, but it is not optional for me. If I were advising you, this would be a mandatory week every year for the rest of your career.

Budget Meeting

This meeting should be set sometime in the middle of November and should only take a few hours. Your first budget meeting may be a much longer and more difficult meeting because you will be doing it for the first time. You will find after years of working through your budget that if you have had a successful pre-budget meeting, this meeting consists of filling in the blanks. During the budget meeting, all those who were responsible for gathering budgetary numbers simply put those numbers in as that item is called out. You may find in the beginning that people question these numbers, and that is healthy. You may also find during the year that these budgetary numbers may be off.

That is because the person who developed that number was mistaken or, in some cases, sloppy. However, after the first few months, you will be able to adjust those numbers. For example, if the rent figure was given as $3,000 per month, but the rent is, in fact, $4,000 per month, that item will be off $1,000 per month resulting in an over budget of $12,000 for the year. Obviously, it would be troubling for the person responsible to miss such an easy target, but you will know after your first month.

In addition to putting your budget together in this final meeting, you will also put your fee projections together for the year. At your pre-budget meeting, you will have asked the lawyers responsible to provide an estimate of fees for next year. You can do this by looking at historical fees or by looking at certain cases or projects for the next year. Fee projection is not as exact as the budget. However, throughout the years, my fee projections are usually very close. I advise being very conservative in your fee projections and very generous in your budget.

We plan this meeting from 9 a.m. to 12 p.m. every year, but I can tell you from firsthand experience that it usually only takes an hour and a half now that we have our systems in place and our people responsible for figures. At the end of this meeting, you will have your budget for the year. Sometimes it absolutely knocks your socks off to see what it costs to run your office. That is the bad news. The good news is, you know exactly what you are facing in the next calendar year. As I have said before, information is power—the good, the bad, and the ugly.

Quarterly Dinner

No matter what the size of your firm, I highly recommend a quarterly dinner be held at the end of every third month. We have quarterly dinners in April, July, and October.

Before the dinner, there is a brief meeting to bring everyone up to speed on what is going on at the firm. While we all lunch together occasionally, there is nothing like a structured dinner to add to the collegial feel of the firm.

We have held these dinners for over fifteen years, and they are a regular staple of our firm. The dinners provide a chance to visit socially outside of work, to develop a bond within the firm, and to catch up on each other's lives. It may seem like a simple thing, but you will be surprised by how long many firms go without breaking bread with one another. I suggest that you place this on your agenda for your first year of treating your business like a business.

Holiday Party

The last calendared event for the year is the holiday party. All employees and their spouses attend. Whether the party is at your home, a restaurant, or a hotel ballroom, there is nothing like bringing the staff together, especially with their spouses. You cannot overestimate the value of thanking spouses for contributing to their other half's work at the firm and to your overall success. I have had these holiday parties for more than twenty years, and because I know spouses and they know me, many employees have remained at the firm for a much longer period that would be the case if I did not.

The firm party establishes your firm as a place of business that values family and appreciates hard work, dedication, and loyalty. The final act for your next calendar year is the holiday party. Make it a ritual, make it fun, and make it forever.

Happy Hour

One more ritual that is not so structured is the happy hour. I have found over the years that calling a firm happy hour that starts at 4:00 p.m. and to ends at 5:30 or 6:00 gives the firm a much-needed boost of adrenaline, energy, and enthusiasm. You cannot underestimate the time spent with staff. They are the people who make or break the success of your firm.

By gathering casually, you show them you care, have fun, and, more importantly, gather information and tidbits you may not have known about. I can't tell you how many things—and I mean important items—I have learned at the firm's happy hour.

You now have the very foundation for building your multi-million-dollar law firm. It is important that all of these events are calendared and followed closely. When you begin to miss any of these meetings, parties, or dinners, you will be on a slippery slope to returning to your old bad habits.

Resolve to treat your firm exactly the way any highly effective business would operate. In this, your law firm should be no different than the community bank, the largest insurance company in your town, or any small business that operates on a high level field. This plan and these habits that you have now adopted will enable you to rise to the next level. For the first time, you will be treating your business like a business. Remember that the best investment you will ever make is in yourself. With that in mind, always remember that a business that is not run like a business is no business at all. At least one that I would never invest in—would you?

It is now time to get more specific and get down to the nitty-gritty in our long-term planning. It is time for bricks and mortar and a foundation that will be a cornerstone for your firm and your future.

I am forever amazed and chagrined when I learn how most law firms run their practices. There are no regularly scheduled meetings, no planning sessions, no budgets or budget meetings. Your most important asset and your greatest stockholding is treated, in many cases, worse than a hotdog stand operator operates his business.

I want you to think about this for a moment. What if one of the companies that you have significant stockholdings in ran its company **exactly** the way you run yours? What if that stock was Oracle? And what if you found out that company never had a board meeting and had no budget or income projections for the coming year? What if you found out the executives and their subordinates never had planning sessions to determine what new products to develop or how to maximize their new sales? What if you found out that instead of having a plan for success, developing a firm culture, and conducting regular sales meetings, these companies just hoped things would work out? What if you found out their meetings consisted of running into each other in the hallways from time to time and going to lunch or out for drinks to discuss events of the day?

I don't think there is a person who would not run out and sell that stock today. You would conclude that Larry Ellison and the Oracle team—while they have done extraordinarily well—have just been plain lucky, and luck is not something to base your future on.

Sadly, for some firms, this is the way they conduct business on a daily basis. Hoping. Wishing. Sometimes gathering hurriedly to put out the latest fire. As obvious as this is for those who plead guilty, it should also be frightening. Your firm may well be in serious trouble, and you are totally unaware of the fact.

As I conclude this chapter, I would like to provide you with some of the structure I have found to be helpful over the last twenty-five plus years. Structures, suggested meetings, and management tools may be helpful to you as you move to more formal business strategy. It has been my experience that these meetings, events, and management tools have been like instruments in a jumbo jet. They force you to pay attention and allow you to see where you are going. They provide you with the data necessary to fly safely, but more importantly, they prepare and alert you in case of an emergency.

9

WHO MOVED MY CHEESE?

Grow or Die

It really doesn't matter which state you live in, the dreaded words "tort reform" have the ability to send shudders down all of our collective spines. I don't know if there is a state in the Union that has not been impacted—some worse than others.

It is hard to fathom all the tort reform that has been implemented in Florida during my legal career. I try not to think what my practice would look like had none of this so-called reform occurred. Sadly, I think of all the people who have not been compensated because the Chamber of Commerce had control of our state government at a certain point in time, and they arbitrarily and capriciously took away fundamental rights. I read that one of these Chamber of Commerce vigilantes was rendered a quadriplegic and the very laws that he bullied through his state house resulted in his devastation. The man now wheels around the country talking about his past sins and the sins still committed against his fellow man and consumers.

All of this tort reform was done under the guise of helping our economy. Here in Florida, when doctors were seeking, in effect, total immunity, they would scream, "If we don't get it, we are moving to another state." I would go to Oregon and hear the same thing. I would go to Pennsylvania and hear the same thing. I would go to Colorado and hear the same thing. I began to ask myself, "Where are they going? Mexico?" Of course not. In the end, it was all political payback in an effort to take away trial lawyers' political muscle and deny money to Democratic pro-consumer candidates.

Unfortunately, as Thomas Frank beautifully pointed out in his book, *What's the Matter with Kansas?*, good people elected politicians who then turned around and harmed them far more than they helped. Under the guise of issues such as abortion, gay rights, and gay marriage, good people inadvertently allowed the United States Chamber of Commerce to take control of their state government. As sad as all of this was and is, the reality is that tort reform has had a dramatic effect on consumer rights and trial lawyer practices throughout this country. Whether fair or unfair, you cannot simply sit back, wring your hands, and say, "Woe is me." Instead, to keep your law practice sustainable, it is important to keep your eye on the ball. One thing that is always certain with American business is that its uncontrolled greed and desire for profits will do things to consumers that will require the trial lawyer's skills.

Think of the Ford Pinto. All of those executives gathered around their conference room and received information about how the Pinto would burst into flames, if struck in a certain way. Their bean counters then presented them with the number of times they thought this would happen and how many people would die or be burnt with different degrees of severity. They were then presented with the probable payout from these "accidents."

As they munched on their salads, they were then presented with numbers that showed what a total recall of **all** Pintos in America and the world would cost Ford. As their mouths fell open and croûtons fell off of their forks, they sat there in utter disbelief. They now had two sets of numbers: the cost of mayhem and death in one column and the cost of recall in another. The decision was easy. They chose mayhem and death. Then they ordered the chef to bring out the filet mignon, au gratin potatoes, and asparagus with just a hint of ginger. Corporate America at work in the 1960s.

This kind of conduct has continued to go on since then and will be going on one hundred years from now. Think of Bernie Madoff, Enron, Tyco, BP, pharmaceutical companies, and manufacturers of medical products here in America. If you sit down at the beach, close your eyes, and try to think of all the examples, you will fall asleep. It is more effective than counting sheep, because there are more instances of this type of terrible abuse than there could ever be sheep in your dreams.

That said, as you begin to take stock of your firm, it is important to do yet another exercise. I don't know if you keep a record of the fees that come in from particular cases, but if you don't, you should. For instance, it is important to know the percentage of cases that generate fees in certain practice areas in your firm. What percentages of personal injury, workers' compensation, or medical malpractice cases constitute your firm's revenue? On a monthly and yearly basis, I can tell you that to the dollar. Remember, information is power.

I suggest you and your partners look back into the last five years and break out your fees and the practice areas from which those fees came. A five-year snapshot can be most illuminating. You will find there are certain practice areas in your firm that you knew were in trouble but were actually on life support. You will see that your firm may well be in decline, or worse—already dying an early death.

Once you have assembled these numbers and taken a look at the past, you will be prepared to move forcefully and competently into the future. I would like for you to read the book *Who Moved My Cheese?* by Spencer Johnson. It will only take about a half hour to do so. It provided me with a different way to look at my business and practice.

The story is fairly simple. There was a city that was great and bountiful. In the center of the city was a seemingly everlasting fountain that produced cheese. Every day, the town's people and mice would come to the city square and grabs hunks of cheese that sustained them for years and years.

One day, when the town's people and mice came to the square, there was no cheese. Days went by with still no cheese. After a few days, the mice knew instinctively that the cheese was most likely never coming back and bolted from the city to the countryside in search of new cheese. Two of the townspeople kept visiting the fountain every single day for weeks and months until they were almost dead. Finally, one of the men told his friend that they had to leave because the cheese was obviously never coming back. One man did so and one man did not. The man that did so had a tough time finding a new source of cheese, but he did. His trip was dangerous and fraught with peril, but he made the trip and saved his life. Although the book never says, you can only assume that the man who never left died slowly of starvation.

When the man finally found the courage to move to a new city, he found not only new cheese, but also more cheese and more selections of cheese. He was flabbergasted at the bounty upon which he now feasted. What he found more stunning was the fact that upon arrival, he discovered two mice from his old city sitting there fat and happy, munching on a batch of Gouda and Muenster. These mice purportedly not as smart as humans, had instinctively known that the cheese was not coming back, and their survival skills kicked in, leading them to a new source of sustenance.

Please buy the book, because my short paragraphs here do not do it justice. This book will illustrate to you, as it did to me, the importance of monitoring your own cheese supply and understanding when that fountain in the town square is on the verge of drying up. For too many firms, the cheese was suddenly gone, even though the slow trickle of the spout clearly indicated that the party was almost over. Because they really didn't want to know or were incapable of facing reality and dealing with the consequences, they instead chose certain death. That's why it's so important for you to take the assessment of your cases, and, by percentage, understand where your fees are coming from. This will help you understand whether that is a growth area in your firm or whether the cheese fountain is almost dry.

A few years ago, nursing home abuse made up about 25 percent of my firm's revenue. It was an untapped market, a loosely regulated industry run in large part by crooks and unethical people. They put our grandparents in warehouses where 40 percent of their workers had a criminal record and kept their eyes solely on profit. It truly was, and is, a human rights issue. Juries were understandably outraged, and verdicts were as powerful as they should have been. The end result was predictable. The United States Chamber of Commerce and their ilk immediately focused an effort to implement tort reform in the nursing home industry, seeking protection for these pillars and titans of American industry. Nursing home executives started setting up shell companies with no insurance and thus no oversight. State legislatures not only passed rounds of tort reform, they did nothing to make these shell corporations accountable. As the result, thousands of America's greatest generation have been abused, neglected, and killed living in institutions tantamount to death camps.

As I watched with my jaw dropped as my own state acted as an accessory to these crimes, I also had to face the reality that this practice area of mine was dying at a very rapid pace. Removing 25 percent of my revenue would decimate my firm. I needed to take action, and I did so, but only because I had implemented the measuring tools necessary to assess the shrinkage in this practice area, and I had the ability to move myself into new areas of law as well as new geographic areas.

Once you and your partners have assessed your practice areas and determined whether those areas are growing or dying, you must decide where you will go in the future. There is no question that the uncertainty will cause you much consternation and second-guessing. However, you only have two alternatives.

Grow or die!

Grow or die has long been my personal mantra for my firm and for all of my other business ventures. It accurately reflects my business philosophy, and, more importantly, all of our species survival instincts. When you embrace the grow or die philosophy, I promise you an empowerment you have not felt in many years, because you must then embrace the methods you will employ to grow your firm. That is when the hard part comes in. Where do we go and how do we get there?

There are essentially two ways to grow your firm:

1. Add new practice areas in your city.

2. Move and expand into new cities.

The only wrong way to grow your practice is not to do so. As part of your responsibility to your firm and family, you and your partners need to sit down and have this discussion. I won't tell you what to do, but I will share with you what I did.

Practice Areas

Over the past five years, I have added new practice areas to my firm. I have one question I ask before jumping into a new area: does this practice area benefit consumers? I don't really focus as much on the profitability but rather the service it will bring. I firmly believe if you focus on money up front, you will make very little. If you focus on servicing consumers and doing good, the money will come. Here are the practice areas I am now involved in that were not even on my radar five to six years ago.

1. Wage and hour/FLSA

2. Mass torts

    a. Pharmaceuticals

    b. Medical devices

3. Consumer class actions

4. Consumer debt

5. Mesothelioma

6. First party

7. Social security disability

8. Commercial contingency

9. Securities and antitrust class actions

10. Qui tam (whistleblower)

Each of these new areas has been adopted after much planning and thought. Each one of these practice areas has a ramp-up time and actually loses money in the short run. However, as you now know, nothing is about today; everything is about tomorrow.

My firm continues to evolve. I understand that in five years, it will look different than it does now. That is life. I also realize some of the practice areas that I have invested in may not pan out. However, I am certain that not doing so would have been far riskier.

In making these growth decisions, there are several things you must consider, and they will make you uncomfortable. If there is a practice area that no one in your firm has supreme confidence in, you must reach outside the firm and hire a section leader. Bringing in new people, especially to run a practice area, makes us all nervous. But once again, the alternative should make you more uncomfortable. You can also move one of your A people into a leadership role in that new practice area. Taking someone who is very profitable and confident in one area and moving them into an unknown area is one sure way to make both of you nervous. Bold moves make us all nervous. Giving up a surefire producer and moving her into the unknown is an excruciating decision. But it is important to have all As heading up these new ventures. If you laterally move a B or a C, your decision is doomed. Don't do it. You'd be better off nibbling on the crumbs of cheese around your desk.

New Geographic Location

Far riskier but with more upside is the decision to move into new cities either as a stand-alone firm or a joint venture. Since Morgan & Morgan opened in 1988, we have opened offices in these cities:

1. Atlanta, GA
2. Naples, FL
3. Orlando, FL
4. Tallahassee, FL
5. Tampa, FL
6. New York, NY
7. Jacksonville, FL
8. Lexington, KY
9. Fort Myers, FL
10. Winter Haven, FL
11. Plantation, FL
12. The Villages, FL
13. St. Petersburg, FL
14. West Palm Beach, FL
15. Jackson, MS
16. Sarasota, FL
17. Kissimmee, FL
18. Lakeland, FL
19. Tavares, FL
20. Nashville, TN
21. Memphis, TN
22. Columbus, GA
23. Daytona Beach, FL
24. Louisville, KY

These are all real offices that are fully staffed and operational. Of the twenty-four offices, one, Phoenix, was actually closed. It wasn't because of a lack of cases; it was because the person I selected to run that office turned out to be the wrong man for the job. I also learned a valuable lesson in having an office thousands of miles away. Today, all of our offices can be reached in two hours or less by jet. Even the failure in Phoenix provided a lesson that has been valuable and will allow me to continue to grow the correct way.

Cities as Joint Ventures

Morgan & Morgan has embarked on joint ventures in these cities:

1. Philadelphia, PA

2. Memphis, TN

3. Washington, DC

4. San Diego, CA

5. Los Angeles, CA

All of these different ventures take on different permutations. Whether we have partnered up with a law firm to give them our technical and trial experience in the nursing home arena or to help them with their wage and hour practice, or we have actually partnered up with local firms to replicate the Morgan & Morgan model, all of the ventures have been profitable or are very close to being profitable.

This chapter could actually be a book or a topic for a three-hour lecture, but hopefully I have provoked you to think about your future in a different way by now. Starting up a new practice area is not without risk. Opening up in a new city is even riskier. But always remember the refrain we were told as children: no guts, no glory. The greater the risk in the decisions you make, the greater the reward will be.

Now that you have had the time to assess your practice areas and your firm, you are left with two courses to take: action or inaction. The choice is yours and yours alone. But before I say yours alone, I should end this chapter with a caveat.

In making the big decisions, your age will most assuredly determine your course of action. Sometimes I see firms that are owned by some partners who are older and some partners who are younger. I have seen firms where the old bull elephant is creeping into retirement and toward sunny days in Boca Raton, Florida where there is no state income tax. Aggressive young lawyers with all the piss and vinegar you could hope for surround him, and their objectives and timetables differ, as does their methodology in going forward. There are many scenarios and different examples I can give, but the common question you must address is this: are my objectives for my future and my family's future compatible with my partner's or my boss's? What is my boss's exit philosophy? Does it include me, or does it just involve him sitting on the beach in Boca Raton and collecting paychecks while I slog through the winters of Detroit, Philadelphia, and Chicago? To leave or not to leave—that is the question.

To answer this question, you really need to spend time and attack it the way you would attack any problem. Except this problem will be one of the most difficult and important decisions you ever make in your life. Again, this is a most uncomfortable process but a most necessary one.

We took an assessment of the past performances of your firm, and we looked into the future. We know what decisions we should make, and now the question is, will we make them? We know we may be working in a place or be partners with people who do not share our business values—or maybe even personal values—and we must make the decision to leave or not to leave. All of these decisions are difficult and that is why, in most cases, we choose to avoid answering them. We choose not to gather all the information I have suggested, and we choose not to ask ourselves what do we do next. Just as we ignore stepping on the scale in the morning, we may choose to ignore looking into the mirror and taking stock of what we see.

The strategies I have suggested must not be taken lightly. If you do, you will continue to operate a petting zoo instead of being the ringmaster at the **greatest show on earth**. Your firm will continue to die a slow death, and even though you may choose not to change things, you now know it is happening. As the cheese gradually disappears from the town square, it is your decision to ignore the dwindling supply or to embrace the challenge that lies ahead. Good luck with your decisions.

Grow or die!

10

SYSTEMS AND GOALS

Study after study has shown that people who have goals do better than people who have no goals and people who write their goals down do significantly better than those goal setters who keep track in their minds. During my business career, I have always written down my goals—not only for myself, but for my coworkers as well. All businesses that you invest in have sales targets every year. Yet it has been my experience that most law firms begin the year with just a wink and a hope that things will work out. My suggestion is to end that type of thinking today.

Just as you must have regular meetings and business sessions, you must put systems and goals in place to reach your full potential. Every two years we are riveted as the Olympics are broadcast into our homes from some city around the world. We watch incredible athletes who have been working their whole lives try to reach their own personal goals or to break world records. These champions spend much time training and preparing, but all of them have certain goals in mind. Whether it was Michael Phelps hitting world record swimming times or the

Dream Team winning a gold medal for basketball, none of these accomplishments could have **ever** occurred unless the athletes had set goals and continually raised bars.

The first thing I suggest you do as you begin a new year is look at all of your producers' historical fees and compare them with others in the firm. No matter how small your firm is—including an office of one—setting goals is essential.

What I further suggest is that you set a goal for yourself and others as you begin to compete in your own personal Olympics. These goals should include the fees you hope to earn in a year, the number of cases you hope to close out in a month, and the number of trials you expect to have.

Because I am a systems person, each and every month I publish these goals with their actual progress and their expected trends at their current paces. For example, if your goal is $1.2 million in fees for the year and you bank zero fees in January, you are trending to be $1.2 million in the negative on your trend line. On the other hand, if you earn $200,000 in fees, you will trend to be up a positive $1.2 million.

We set and publish these goals on a monthly basis for all of the attorneys in our firm. Money is a wonderful motivator, but over the years, I have found competition and pride are sometimes as important as money itself. I can tell you firsthand that the lawyers whose names appear at the bottom of the monthly report are as bothered by this fact as they are by the lack of bonuses for their efforts.

In our personal injury department, we expect a lawyer who handles litigation to have between sixty and eighty cases in litigation at any given time, and those who are primarily handling pre-suit to have an inventory of between 120 and 140 files. We have experimented with all types of case counts, but we have found that once a person has too many cases, they get to the point of diminishing return. Although it may make sense to think a person with 200 cases would produce more fees than a person with 130 cases, the opposite has proven to be true. Instead of being proactive they become reactive, and instead of doing positive things, they put fires out all day long. It has been my experience that a lawyer predominantly handling presuit files with a case load of 120 to 130 cases should be expected to close six cases a month. If they do so, their results will be outstanding. As part of our goals, we also publish the number of cases our attorneys have closed and how close they are to the target of seventy-two cases per year. That is set as a firm wide goal. Here, you will find some of the forms that allow our lawyers to measure their progress, and compare themselves with other people in their practice areas. These systems must be published at the first of every month. You will find if you buy into these systems, setting goals will become a fundamental part of your firm's culture.

Moving cases in presuit is important, but the litigation process is even more so. One of the common mistakes I have witnessed in and outside of my firm is the way a case of magnitude is handled when it first comes into the firm. Your next exercise is to take a look at all of the cases you, and your firm, settled last year. Write them down on a piece of paper and with the total settlement and the fees. You will be surprised to find the occurrence of what I call the 80/20, 20/80 rule. You will find that about 20 percent of your cases resulted in 80 percent of your total fees. More alarming is the fact that because of a lack of focus, systems, and proper goal setting, 80 percent of a lawyer's time is spent working on 20 percent of your firm's fees. Let me tell you why.

We get into the habit of treating all of our cases exactly alike. A case with soft tissue injuries comes in, and in many firms it is handled in the same way as a serious death case. It is vital that practice ends today.

My suggestion is that every case of magnitude be separated and triaged much differently than run-of-the-mill cases. Also, cases with difficult liability but severe injuries should be handled different than run-of-the-mill cases. It is my suggestion that you ask this question every time you look at one of these files: do I expect to ever settle this case in presuit for a fair amount of money for my client? If the answer is no, you need to file suit. Too often,

I find lawyers monkeying around with such cases for nine, ten, or eleven months instead of doing what they know needs to be done from the outset—file suit! Why wait ten months and put your client further behind the eight ball? We know from experience that the older a case gets, the worse it gets. We also know that early investigation and early discovery is key.

All of us have been fired one time or another in our career. I am sure you remember the times you were fired from the cases with big injuries and great coverage. I will promise you that you will **never** be fired from any case if that case is in litigation. It's simply doesn't happen. It doesn't happen because you are engaged with the client and that client knows he or she has your full attention.

If you distinguish the cases of magnitude from those that should be handled in presuit at the front end of your case evaluation, you will begin to firmly establish what is known as the 80/80 rule. That means you will spend 80 percent of your time working on cases that will yield 80 percent of your fees. You will conduct a much more thorough initial investigation and witness-taking exercise. Your discovery will be more thorough than you ever hoped for, and your clients will benefit in ways you never could have imagined. Finally, your firm will be more successful as you change the way you work. You are now working smart instead of putting out fires.

I have spent a career building systems to effectively move presuit cases. I could write a book on that subject alone. However, I would like to offer you a present at this juncture of the book. If you would like to receive all of my forms and the systems I have put together, simply go to www.trialguides.com/resources/downloads/you-cant-teach-hungry. You can download all of our forms and systems for you to utilize in your own practice. I certainly understand that since I am in Florida, there may be items that are not relevant to your state, but these are forms we use in all of the states where we do business (Florida, Mississippi, Georgia, Tennessee, California, Kentucky, Washington, DC, Maryland and Virginia).

You can tweak these forms and systems as your situation dictates, and I hope the letters and systems I have developed over the past twenty-five years prove helpful. The systems have basically been developed over time to help me expedite our presuit cases. More importantly, many of the letters, forms, and procedures were developed after a near calamity or a brush with legal malpractice. I hope they help. I promise you that I am giving you my holy grail and the key to one of our longtime successes—the presuit case.

I also want to talk about a system that is extremely important to all of our offices. In my offices in Florida, we call it our ten-month report. In other states, depending on the statute of limitations, we implement shorter time frames.

In Florida, general negligence cases have a four-year statute of limitation, which can be a blessing and a curse. The curse comes when a lawyer decides to go into full-blown procrastination mode and wakes up three and a half years after intake to realize they have done little to nothing on a certain file and legal malpractice is burning right under their desk.

Each month, our lawyers meet with their legal assistants and conduct a ten-month report meeting. Every case in their inventory that has been in their office for ten months or longer is physically brought to this meeting. The question is very simple for every case. Why is this case still in presuit, and why have they not filed suit? Many times, there are very good reasons. But as often as not, it is because the case has not been pushed properly, and we have allowed it to languish. For each case remaining on the list, lawyers must fill out a report that explains, preferably in one sentence, why this case is remaining or what the action plan is.

We also include a key number on this ten-month report—the number of months a case has been on the report. For example, if a case has been on the report for thirteen months, that case has been in the firm, in presuit, for twenty-three months. That is a problem. And that doesn't even take into account that a case may have come to us months after the subject accident; the statute of limitations clock has an even shorter time frame than the twenty-three months that it shows.

This ten-month report system and meeting is mandatory in all of our offices. You will find that using this ten-month report system and having a regularly scheduled meeting on your calendar to produce a report, even if it is just for yourself, will enable you to fully embrace and employ the 80/80 rule. I promise you will see a difference. Implementing systems, setting goals, and writing those goals down has made all the difference in our law firms. However, the systems only work if they are followed—if the meetings are held, if the reports are prepared monthly, and, most importantly, if the results are circulated for everyone to see. Never underestimate peer pressure, and never underestimate goals, especially written goals.

11

BACK OF THE HOUSE

The Devil is in the Details

Please pay close attention to this chapter. I promise the things you learn here will make you hundreds of thousands of dollars in the short run and millions of dollars in the long run. The things you will find in this chapter are the most overlooked by law firms for reasons I find hard to understand.

Many firms market themselves, have business development lunches, try cases, and get results, but I find it glaringly lacking that little attention is paid to the back of the house. As the old saying goes, the devil is in the details.

Let me give you a few jewels that will probably cause you to put this book down and go off and investigate.[6] We spend time and effort developing a name and reputation, but have you **ever** called directory assistance or searched online for your firm and

---

6. I hope this turns out to be the kind of book that you want to pick up again once you put it down.

phone number? Have you ever called directory assistance, asked for your name, and determined whether or not it is listed? Have you ever called directory assistance in the city that you work in to determine if **all** of the lawyers in your firm are listed in directory assistance? Believe it or not, the associates in your firm have developed a network of potential sources. Remember that the directory assistance operator most likely makes close to minimum wage and has a quota for the number of calls they need to answer. That is the type of employee that may be determining whether the million-dollar case that is desperately trying to contact you receives the correct number.

About seven years ago, I formed a marketing company to advise, consult, and produce advertising for lawyers throughout America. It is called Practice Made Perfect or PMP. In almost every instance, we found our potential clients had paid little or no attention to this very, very large detail. In many cases, we found clients that had their primary offices in suburbs sitting outside of big cities, but no listings for their firm, themselves, or their associates in any of the surrounding cities. They simply had to hope that the directory assistance operators would broaden their searches.

Now, if this little drill hasn't driven you crazy yet, what if you are a person whose name has an odd spelling or multiple spellings? Is it Stine or Stein? Is it Cook or Kuck? Is it Kelly or Kelley? Why is this important? It is essential that directory assistance operators not only have the correct spelling of your name but alternative spellings as well. It costs nothing in most cities or pennies at the most. For those of you with impossible names like Steve Schwartzapfel,

Ed Zebersky, and Frank Piscitelli, your challenge has just begun. It is not only incumbent upon you to make sure your name is listed, but you must also consider that there may be many alternative phonetic ways to find your name in directory assistance. This overlooked exercise can cost firms and individuals millions of dollars during their career. It happens because we focus on what we think may be important and the obvious sometimes escapes us. Remember, only the paranoid survive.

The next thing I would like you to do is to search online for your firm name, your own name, and the names of every member of your firm. Again, for many of you the results will be shocking. You won't show up. Your firm might not show up. Your associates probably won't show up. You will immediately think, "My God, how long has this been going on, and how much business have I lost?" Remember, we are planting new trees today. Get your shovel out.

Another detail that many of the firms with whom I have consulted overlook is the emphasis on a strong and reliable receptionist. My receptionist has been with me in my Orlando office since I first set up my own shop. Because she is smart, because she cares, and because we love each other, my business matters to her. Too often, I find firms that swap receptionists out like they are pumpkin seeds, easily chewed and spit out. Yet, these people are the gatekeepers of your kingdom. If it's 4:59 p.m., they have gathered their bags to leave, and the phone rings, they may just walk out. If they care about you, they won't. Throughout my organization, we pay much attention to the hiring of our receptionist. When you are doing your retention of service survey, pay close attention to the receptionist position. If you have a revolving door there, you have a big problem—a problem so big that quantifying the amount of money you have lost from it is impossible.

The other common flaw I find in personal injury firms is that there is no procedure for getting new and prospective clients to the proper person to handle their matter. I own Marriott Hotels throughout America, and we often survey our guests and shop our hotels. Likewise, I would suggest that you and your partners shop your firm. Find out exactly what *really* goes on when a prospective client calls your firm. We shop our own firm hundreds of times a year.

When you shop your firm, you may become aware of one of two things:

1. You have no procedure for handling new client calls.

2. The procedure has long since been abandoned and your business is in a free fall.

A new client call is one of the details I pay particular attention to. When a client decides to call your firm, they are ready to hire you. They are no different than the customer who calls a plumber with a plumbing problem when their septic tank has backed up. When you call the plumber, you don't expect to hear, "I'll call you back," or be kept on hold for five minutes. When you call the plumber, you expect to hear, "We will be at the house in two hours." I hope you run your business like a plumber and not like a lawyer from this point forward.

If your firm is still in the Dark Ages and writing new cases down on pink sheets that a lawyer or legal assistant will follow up on when they are good and ready, you are costing yourself millions of dollars. If you are passing new clients through to a voicemail that may not be answered until a lawyer concludes his trial or vacation, you are losing millions of dollars. If you do not have a call center procedure for new cases that come to your office, the amount of money that you and your partners are losing on an annual basis may be too much to be calculated.

As you begin to plant new trees in your firm, I strongly recommend developing procedures for handling potential new clients. If I could only give one piece of advice as to my success, it would be my maniacal focus on new cases that call into our office and the way we handle them.

In developing my systems, I conducted extensive tests and interviews with case management software developers. After spending a great deal of time investigating, I developed case management systems and call center systems that would do the best job, far and away, for a personal injury firm. Our call center system captures information and data that is vital to your firm's success. This software also has the capability to make referrals and track those referrals with tickler systems that allow the process to move without human hands. These systems are so important to my business, and we now have begun to commercially market these web-based programs that I promise will make all the difference in your practice in the long run.

Unless you have designated people to take in new cases and potential new clients always speaks to a live person, you will continue to lose money. I cannot emphasize this fact enough. When a new client calls Morgan & Morgan, they are immediately placed with an intake specialist who then gets their information, downloads it, and, most importantly, **sets the appointment**.

Setting an appointment, whether at your office or at their home, is the most important thing you can do in making sure that client goes nowhere else. When you call Roto-Rooter and they tell you they will be there at 1:00 p.m., you stop calling plumbers. Even if the Roto-Rooter representative calls you at 1:00 p.m. and says they are running late, you may be upset, but you still wait for them to get there.

You must utilize a designated person, even if it is just your administrative assistant. Setting the appointment ensures the sign-up. Remember, even when I only had two lawyers, I always had one person designated to take in new client calls on a full-time basis. Look at it this way—if you pay someone $30,000 a year but their sole job is to talk to new clients, you only need one case to justify that expense. More importantly, there will be hundreds of small cases that could potentially slip through the cracks. I have found when firms implement a rotation of lawyers, staff, or paralegals to handle calls from potential new clients, it is like passing a hot potato around the kitchen. Nobody wants to take it. When it is **your job** and you become responsible, everything changes.

I realize some of you will not take this leap, and that is fine too. But please make sure that someone, even if it is your administrative assistant, responds to new cases before returning all other phone calls. If you prioritize this as part of your office, you will be seeing and signing up more new clients.

Here are a few final thoughts about your intake process for you to consider:

1. Are you satisfied with the way new cases are being screened when the office is closed?

2. How does the call service work at night and on the weekends?

3. Is the client contacted and scheduled at night or on the weekends?

4. Is someone in charge of assuring your phone numbers are properly listed in the directory assistance in your local areas?

5. Who is responsible for your website and your name appearing properly when searched?

I cannot begin to overemphasize the importance of the back of the house. Without giving attention to this often-overlooked area of your law firm, it will never be the firm it could be. A strong and loyal receptionist is your firm's guardian. The failure to have a proper, accountable intake for clients is a slippery slope that will cost you millions of dollars and thousands of potential new clients. If you don't shop your firm from time to time to understand if your procedures are being followed, you will never know if the tree you planted three years ago is no longer receiving fertilizer and water.

Please resolve to treat this part of your business as if you were a plumber from this day forward. The toilet is stopped up. The customer has called for help. How long will the customer wait for you to respond and make that appointment? Finally, remember that setting an appointment stops the music. The client is satisfied but only if you are going to make a trip to their home or set up an appointment in your office.

I have called this process catching crumbs in my firm. By catching all of the crumbs that fall off of most firm's tables every day, I am able to assemble those crumbs, mash them together, put them in the oven, and pull out a luscious loaf of bread.

The devil is in the details, and if you don't pay attention, you will soon find your firm slipping and sliding. Remember this: your competition may not be as lackadaisical as you are.

12

ADVERTISING 101

Just Hoping Doesn't Work

All modesty aside, there is probably not a lawyer in America who knows more about legal advertising than me. I graduated from law school in 1982, five years after *Bates vs. Arizona*. In those early years, only the most rogue attorneys dared to advertise on TV. They were shunned and looked down upon. They were, in short, viewed as pariahs. Lawyers who could afford to advertise wouldn't, and lawyers who would advertise couldn't afford to. During those early years, I went to the local firms that had ventured into advertising and received many of their referrals. I placed myself in the belly of the beast.

Not only did I see that the phone was ringing as a result of advertising, but I also saw that some pretty darn good cases were coming through the door. By 1988, I had ventured off with one of my associates and began to advertise myself. I felt what Barry Bonds must have felt when he saw a big fastball coming down the middle of the plate. I knew just what the future held and decided to swing with all of my might. We started with an advertising budget of $100,000 a year, COD. We never looked back. Because of the disdain other lawyers had for advertising, it was like a hole had opened up on the football field, I had run a draw play from my own end zone, and there was nothing but clear sailing in front of me. Today, I operate law offices throughout America and spend between $35–40 million a year on advertising, depending on whether I have mass tort or specialty projects ongoing. It is a long way from $100,000 COD.

I could write a textbook on this subject, but, instead, I will give you some high points and some common mistakes I have seen other firms make.

I see law firms begin to advertise with no clear goals, no budget, and inadequate capital. In most cases, they are led by advertising agencies or media buyers who do not have their best interests at heart. This, much to my firm's benefit, is a common mistake.

I have seen many competitors come and go, and the scenario is usually very similar. When the ads begin, the quality is spectacular. The firm spent tens of thousands of dollars on two or three ads and was totally ripped off by its advertising agency, which said, "Image is everything, and we must create an ad that makes you stand out." Total hogwash and very close to grand larceny.

The next thing that usually happens is that these ads run at the wrong times, to the wrong audience, and often when the back of the house is not prepared to handle new clients. I then watch these poor souls pour money down a rathole, and after four or five months, they have concluded that advertising does not work and they would just as soon not be known as advertising lawyers anyway. Smarting from the loss of anywhere between $150,000 and $300,000, the firm spends the rest of the next couple of years digging out of this ill-conceived hole.

Let me say as forcefully as I can—**advertising works!** To understand that, you just have to look around your own communities and look at the lawyers who have done it so effectively for so many years. You just have to look at the advertising budgets of all of the companies that trade on the New York Stock Exchange (and look at their advertising budget) to understand that not only is advertising working, it is essential. Watch the political campaigns and understand that political candidates win and lose based on the money they have collected for one purpose and one purpose only: advertising.

Advertising is one of the main tools you must utilize to develop a sustainable law firm. It provides you with a way to grow your business and to avoid deep, deep valleys when, for whatever reason, your cases don't come in the way you expected them to or you don't receive that **one** big case that would get you over the hump year in and year out. The truth is, your next-door neighbors can only be killed by Walmart trucks every three or four years. The implementation of a cohesive advertising program is one of the key steps in building a multimillion-dollar law firm. It ensures you have a plan and takes you from merely hoping to actually doing.

While I know there are some very successful firms that do not rely on advertising, they are few and far between, and I would suggest that many of them—especially in the mass tort and class action arena—simply use other firms to do their bidding. They do this so that they can walk into the law conventions with their ribbons on and discuss the disgraceful advertising of so many of their peers. Behind all of these national campaigns you see on cable are prestigious law firms that "do not advertise." Don't be fooled. This is a new day with new realities and a new generation of lawyers who grew up watching attorney advertising and think nothing of it. Advertising no longer carries the stigma it had in the 1980s.

Once you have made the decision to advertise, the mediums you choose to utilize will be critical, and you must lay out a practical twelve-month plan.

As I mentioned earlier, because I saw such a need for this service, I developed my own advertising agency, Practice Made Perfect. I am proud to have helped so many fellow lawyers build a sustainable law firm with an action plan, a flow of cases, and strategies to help them going forward. If you would like to receive information concerning our agency, contact me at jmorgan@forthepeople.com and I will have the appropriate people get in touch with you.

A new client budget really all depends on the amount of money that firm is willing to put into a program and how much money they are willing to borrow. Whenever I mention the word borrow, most prospective clients look at me as if I have three eyes. The prospect of borrowing from a bank has never crossed their minds. I think law firms must be the only businesses in America that have this illusion. Car dealers, gas stations, and furniture stores all borrow money to buy inventory and resell it. This concept of borrowing money to bring inventory into your store is not a novel concept. The risk in this instance, though, is that the inventory may not come. I am here to tell you I have never seen the inventory not come except where there was no budget, no plan, and inadequate capital secured up front. And I mean **never**.

Because traditional advertising agencies don't understand what goes on inside a personal injury law firm, they do not know how to make a smart buy. For example, we know from experience that if you choose to advertise on television, you should front-load your ads on Monday, and, depending on your budget, run far fewer ads on Friday. Why is this? Because Monday is a day when people are ready to take action. It is a day that we know historically results in many more phone calls than Friday. We also know from experience that as the week progresses, even with a constant amount of money being spent on those weekdays, the number of potential cases decreases. That is why we suggest that clients who have a budget buy only Monday through Wednesday. If you are going to go fishing, fish when and where they are biting.

Television

If you were to ask me today where should I advertise, my answer would most certainly be television first, second, and third. Simply put, it works. However, the placement of your ads is critical, and the way you buy your ads can mean the difference in you paying three, four, or, in some cases, even ten times as much as your competitor because you don't know any better.

In buying ads, as I've said before, I'd load up on Monday and decrease as the week progresses, depending upon my budget. I would also run ten-second ads during the news and primetime, where you will be talking to people not within your daytime audience. Most lawyers operate under the dated idea that advertising should be done between 9 a.m. and 4 p.m. while people who are hurt are glued in front of the TV watching reruns of *The Andy Griffith Show* and *Barney Miller*. That was then; this is now. In developing your television rotation, it's important to remember that you're not just at the carnival for one night hoping to win the gigantic stuffed animal and go home. You are in the process of branding yourself and your firm in a way that will provide sustenance to your firm for the rest of your career. This is not a one-trick pony. This is the building of a brand. Ten-second ads during morning news, evening news, and primetime begin to get into the psyche of the consumers in your area.

I believe very strongly that before you advertise, you need to have a branding statement that will be with you for the rest of your career. I end every ad I have ever run with my slogan, "For the People." Likewise, it is important you have an easily navigable website and an easy-to-remember domain name. Mine is www.forthepeople.com. If you do not spend much time coming up with these two key ingredients, you will be throwing money off the bridge, and you will be forced to come back later and tinker with what should have been done at the beginning. Remember, if you are going to do it right, do it right the first time.

Another thing I will tell you about television is that the month of January proves to be fertile ground while the month of December is fallow. For that reason, I never advertise in December. Use December to work your files, get cases settled or put them into litigation, and prepare yourself for the New Year. Once you have your firm name established, your branding statement set in stone, and your domain name for a website determined, you are ready to be turned loose on the world of television.

It is important you have a twelve-month strategy—one that you must understand is going to give you a lot of heartburn. When I opened up my office in southwest Florida, I went there with a million-dollar budget! After the first three months, I had not signed up one new client. I had received calls, but not one new client. Panic set in. I became concerned that the phone lines were not working, and as I had entered my fourth market, I began to understand what others must go through when times like this hit. However, because I had a budget and a time frame, I kept doing exactly what the book told me to do. By summer, the cases were coming in, and by the end, of the year I knew I had a winner. Had I not had this budget and this plan, I can easily see how I might have pulled the plug at the end of March, taken my $333,000 loss, and gone home to lick my wounds. I cannot overemphasize the need for commitment to a twelve-month period of advertising. If you do not have the commitment or the money for that, do not begin.

The next thing I must emphasize about television advertising—and really all advertising—is what we talked about in the previous chapter. If your back of the house is not fully operational, you are throwing money away. If the receptionist is not prepared, intake procedures are not uniform, tracking systems are not in place, and procedures to handle calls that come in after hours or on the weekends are lacking, launching your program is a tremendous mistake. Too many times, I have seen law firms focus on the front-end, the production of the ad, and the excitement of being in front of the camera and seeing themselves on *SportsCenter* for the first time, while they are totally unprepared for what is coming next. It reminds me of the *I Love Lucy* episode where Lucy tries to package chocolates coming too fast off an assembly line. At the end of the day, you will be standing knee-deep in ruined chocolates.

While I am on the subject of *SportsCenter*, let me give you some very key advice. When I advertise, I primarily place focus on the female demographic for two reasons. The first is that even though I have found the mix of our clients skews more heavily toward men than women, I have also found that the person who initiates the call is, more often then not, the wife. In the book *Womenomics,* authors Claire Shipman and Katty Kay conclude that women make 80 percent of a household's consumer decisions. Women run the show. It's hard to admit, but it's a fact.

The second reason is the way men and women watch television. Men watch television like a Doberman on a lunge line. Sitting on the edge of their chair with a remote control glued to their hand, they have one goal and one goal only—never, ever watching a commercial. When women watch television, they nest. When women watch TV, they are there for the long haul, and they resent any man who decides he is going to be watching TV in that same room with the remote control in his hand. Commercials are a backdrop to women, and women don't mind them. In fact, they often enjoy them. I strongly suggest against making an error I see so many times—buying sports ads because you like sports and can't wait to see yourself on the halftime report during the game. It's money down a drain.

To reiterate, when you first begin to advertise, television should make up a significant part of your overall strategy and budget. How you allocate your dollars in large part will depend upon the strategy laid out for you by your advertising agency. Be very careful when you hire your advertising agency, because that one decision may prove to be the best or worst decision you make in your entire career.

Yellow Pages

There is probably not one form of advertising that is more reviled by lawyers and businesspeople than the yellow pages. For our entire business careers, they have held us hostage. They continue to increase the size of ads to the point that in some cities, the largest ad is three full pages. Of course, the larger the ad, the closer you are to the front of the heading. Fortunately, the advent of the internet is causing the yellow pages serious (and life-threatening) heartburn. Until recently, I spent millions of dollars a year on yellow page advertising. I was too scared not to. The yellow pages remind me of season tickets I once had for a pro sports franchise that was a world-class team when I bought them but deteriorated into an abysmal group of slackers over the years. Those tickets had been worth so much to me that losing my aisle seat at center court was almost more than I could bear. However, the day I finally mustered the courage to say I didn't want them anymore was one of the most liberating in my life. I have publicly declared the yellow pages dead! Recently, a colleague and close friend of mine who had been a long-time yellow-page advertiser asked me for advice. I told him to get rid of his yellow pages and move all of the money to TV because he was on a limited budget. The results have been astounding. He has tripled the number of new cases since making this move. It is a bold move, but one that needs to be made. When I moved away from the yellow pages, I never looked back.

Billboards

I am a great proponent of billboards. It gives you top-of-mind awareness, and, over time, it becomes ingrained into the minds of the people of your city. It is a form of advertising many lawyers don't like because it does not give them immediate gratification— ad goes up, caller calls in, case signed up.

The billboard is for the long-term thinkers, the person and firm that is planning for the next twenty to thirty years. As one of the first law firm users of billboards in the country, I am convinced that my billboard campaign has been greatly beneficial to me and greatly detrimental to my competitors.

Radio

For many years, I have bought of radio ads. I liked the radio because messages could be more detailed and target audiences more precise. I still use radio a great deal. However, satellite radio and other technology such as Pandora allows users to move channel to channel at the speed of sound or forgo radio completely, and that makes radio a more challenging buy. I am still buying it, but with a guarded eye.

The Purple Cow

I am constantly looking for advertising opportunities that allow me to be the one person in my group who stands out. I call it the purple cow. Purple cow advertisements are things such as cab tops; five- and ten-second ads between songs on the radio; or weather and traffic sponsorships on television, radio, and even blimps. Billboards also fall into this category.

When I talk about purple cow advertising, I am talking about advertising that is impossible or near impossible to miss. I am looking for avenues of advertising that the local consumer can miss only if they drive with their eyes shut and ears plugged. I am looking for openings where even that male viewer sitting in his Barcalounger like a Doberman on a lunge line does not have time to miss my ad.

It is a technique I have used successfully, as have our Practice Made Perfect clients.

Internet

Where, oh where do I begin? The internet is here; it is frustrating and confounding, but it is your future. The internet is like television was in the 1950s. If you aren't already familiar with it, you are going to have to learn to navigate this beast because the younger generations will and likely already have.

There is so much to say on this subject that I won't even attempt to say it all in this book. I will say that if you do not know terms such as search engine optimization, pay-per-click, white hat, black hat, expectation-maximization algorithm, organic and inorganic searches, and long-tail searches, you are in for a world of hurt. You need to make a conscientious effort today to begin to understand this new world.

The most frustrating part of the internet is that there are so many so-called experts out there ready and willing to take our money and feed us mush. It is like determining the difference between cubic zirconia and diamonds. At Morgan & Morgan, we have a team of twelve very well compensated people who spend every waking moment optimizing our website, bidding on pay-per-click terms, and providing content and links to our site. At the time of my first revision of this book, pay-per-click rules and search engine algorithms have drastically changed from when I first wrote it, and we have adapted to these changes. More consumers are searching the internet on smartphones abandoning direct internet searches completely in favor of social media apps. We are constantly learning and dealing with these trends. At Practice Made Perfect, we have been able to help our clients navigate these tricky waters.

The final suggestion I will make concerning the internet and your incoming calls is to make sure you harvest and keep every email address that you can. It does not matter whether it is from an inquiry on the internet or a call to your office. We use these email addresses to create a very formidable database that allows us to communicate with former clients and people who have shown an interest in our firm. To be able to punch one button and deploy a database of people who are disposed favorably to your firm is an enormous plus. Make sure you begin to collect and build your database today.

No matter what you decide to do regarding the internet, do something. The internet is with us for good, or at least for the duration of our practice. The way it is integrated into advertising programs is tremendously important to the future of your sustainable law firm. At Morgan & Morgan, we direct potential clients to our website in almost every television and radio ad.

I know I have touched ever so slightly on this topic of advertising. I have twenty-five years of tremendous mistakes and missteps that would take me more time to write than the Bible. The point that I am trying to make, however, is that without an advertising program, you will never build the type of law firm that will be sustainable. I know this is a very dramatic statement, but it is one that I believe. I know there may be a few firms out there that don't advertise and are successful. However, for the rest of us, this is advice that should be heeded. But remember, when you take this advice and go forward, if your back of the house is not prepared, don't bother. It is no good to have a beautiful restaurant with beautiful furnishings if you do not have a kitchen with chefs and waiters.

13

The Black Swan

You may have noticed that many of the chapters in this book use titles of certain books. I have read these books over the years. Each of the books that form the title of a chapter in my own book have been very important to me in the development of my business life, personal life, and family life.

Recently, I read a book by Nassim Nicholas Taleb called *The Black Swan: The Impact of the Highly Improbable*. It is an important book for you to read in its entirety, but I want to give you the gist of it and my take on the consequences and benefits of its lessons to you and your firm. Much of what I have written in the preceding chapters has to do with formulas that have worked for me time and again, year in and year out. These formulas and business practices are invaluable to me as I move forward. They have given me a road map for my future endeavors, and I have relied upon them repeatedly. However, as valuable as the past is and as valuable as past successes are, they can be dangerous in many cases and, in some cases, lethal.

We are all creatures of this earth and creatures of habit. The more we know about certain things, the more certain we become. Because things always seem to work out when we push levers and buttons, we believe they will continue to work out when we push those same buttons and levers over and over again. In short, the more we know, the more certain we are to believe it will happen again and will continue forever. Years ago, when people were first asked what color swans were, their answer was firm and decisive. Swans are white. The longer that man was on this earth, the more firm and decisive this answer became. The answer was given with such certainty because in the history of mankind, no one had ever seen a black swan.

One day while enjoying a beautiful spring day in the woods, a couple came upon a serene lake. Out of nowhere, two swans appeared. Much to the consternation, surprise, and bewilderment of the couple, these were not two ordinary swans. They were not ordinary because they were black swans! The man, a biologist, became flabbergasted. He was able to capture the birds, examine the birds, and discover that despite all of his years of training as a biologist and despite all of the textbooks and literature he had read, certainty had suddenly become uncertain.

It had become incumbent upon him to report to the world that swans were both white and black. Fortunately for mankind and civilization, this revelation had little effect other than that of surprise. The lesson, however, is one that should have become indelible for all future citizens of this world. Since white swans were all we ever knew about, it was all we thought was possible. The longer it was the rule of nature, the longer we believed it to be infallible.

The more we know, the more we think we know. And the more we think we know, the more certain we become in our belief. Even though this black swan lesson occurred in nature and even though black swans occur in business, our personal lives, and nature every single year, we never learn the lesson. The lesson of the black swan is the most important one you will need to learn as you begin to build your firm. Black swans have come at us through the ages. Most troubling and disconcerting about a black swan event is that we never see it coming. The Great Depression was a black swan. Up until the Great Depression, it seemed that America was invincible. Company profits were off the charts. Prosperity was rampant. The good times rolled and would roll forever.

Never in a million years did America or the world see Black Friday coming. On that day, everything changed forever. Unemployment rose to 25 percent. Businesspeople jumped out of buildings. Soup kitchens were formed to provide nourishment to former white-collar businesspeople and their families. Hoovervilles, cities made up of boxes, sprang up throughout America. We never saw it coming!

From 1991 until mid 2008, America forgot the lessons of the Great Depression. It went something like this: you place money in the stock market. No matter what stocks or funds you buy, you make a minimum return of 10 to 12 percent a year. Even though P/E ratios were at unsustainable and obscene highs, we all blindly poured money into 401(k)s like pigs at the trough.

It was not uncommon to go to private clubs and see mortgage brokers and stockbrokers hotboxing a businessperson, promising them a can't-lose strategy. It went something like this: "We are going to refinance your home and move hundreds of thousands of dollars into the stock market. You will receive tax benefits on your home mortgage and pay only 4 or 5 percent on your interest rate. We will then take that money and give it to this friendly stockbroker, who will invest it in the can't-lose stock market. Depending on the funds or stocks that he picks, you will receive an annualized return of between 12 and 14 percent. You will be making an extra 6 to 8 percent a year on your money, and by the time you retire, you will have a few extra million dollars that you never would have had but for this lunch."

The mortgage broker took obscene commissions for the refinance. The stockbroker, who had as much skill as a chimpanzee with a dartboard in most cases, took obscene commissions for throwing darts blindly into the night. Many couples carved out some "extra" money for themselves for home improvements because doing so would add value to their homes. Don't forget it was also "certain" that home prices would rise between 7 and 10 percent a year as well. With this "certainty" at their disposal, people made home improvements and built McMansions throughout the United States.

Mortgage brokers got rich. Stockbrokers got rich. Homebuilders got rich. Interior decorators got rich. And let's not forget the retailers.

Because the good times were rolling so fast, many of these same couples kept a few thousand dollars to buy essential baubles such as Gucci purses, exotic vacations, alligator shoes, and anything that Neiman Marcus threw at us in its Christmas catalog.

For seventeen years, all we saw were white swans.

It is really not necessary to spend much time recapping how the story ended. Stock prices were cut in half. Home values tumbled. Exotic adjustable rate mortgages kicked in, and hundreds of thousands of people lost their homes. Retirement plans were decimated. College funds were depleted. People lost jobs at alarming rates. Homes stood half-built. Subdivisions became tumbleweed towns. The courts could not keep up with foreclosures. The secure lives people once knew were ravaged. People's futures, hopes, and dreams were shattered. Most importantly, certainty was no longer certain.

Mortgage brokers who had made six-figure incomes worked as waiters at Bennigan's—and then Bennigan's filled for bankruptcy. Real estate agents who had raced around town in Mercedes convertibles now raced to the courthouse while their own homes were foreclosed on. They left their Gucci bags behind; it would have been bad form. Stockbrokers who knew less about picking stocks than Koko the gorilla now sat glued in front of their computers browsing www.monster.com.

As we watched our world crumble before us, we had one constant and recurring thought: are **we** heading into the second Great Depression?

Please excuse the following political editorial. Mercifully, Barack Obama was elected president. He surrounded himself with smart people who implemented strategies that halted the skid in the short run and gave us some minor upticks. Even now, most of America is shell-shocked from what happened, and certainty is no longer certain. It turned out that we did not heed the lessons from those black swans years ago, nor had the lessons we had learned from generation to generation been remembered.

Black swans don't simply come as financial tsunamis, but, in some cases, they come as true tsunamis. When you sit on a beautiful beach sipping mai tais and munching on coconut shrimp at a resort in Indonesia, you are not supposed to be whisked away in seconds by the seas and killed along with 250,000 other people. A young father on his morning jog is not supposed to keel over and die from a heart attack. Mothers are not supposed to be killed in traffic accidents while taking their children to school. Children are not supposed to develop fatal diseases and be buried by their parents. It is not normal. It should not happen. However, let this chapter be the constant reminder that black swans are around us in our daily lives. They are flying overhead, but we just don't know it. Does the young father or the young mother taken from us so tragically have life insurance? Should there have been warning systems in Indonesia that would have tipped the government off about a pending tsunami? Had we taken that child in for tests earlier, could the fatal disease been discovered and avoided?

As you read this chapter, you may be wondering just as I wondered when I read *The Black Swan*: what is there to be done? It is certain that the more we know, the more we behave a certain way. And the longer things are the same, the more certain we become. So the ultimate question in life and in business is, what is the answer for the black swan?

The answer is two words. **Be prepared!**

As you approach life and as you begin to build your law firm, you must be aware of these hidden sinkholes that are around every corner. You must prepare your business for the surprise or the unlikely. At the end of the day, it turns out that it is not what we know that matters, but what we don't know.

I repeat: **it is not what we know that matters, but what we don't know.**

Fortunately for me, the Great Recession was not as traumatic as it was for most people. Let me tell you why, and let me tell you what I suggest for you both personally and professionally. I want to give you a list of what I call John's commandments.

JOHN'S COMMANDMENTS

I.   Pay off all consumer debt and car debt before investing in the stock market.

II. Pay off your home and second home before investing in the stock market.

III. Read a book titled *A Random Walk Down Wall Street: The Time-Tested Strategy for Successful Investing* by Burton G. Malkiel, and follow that investment strategy to the letter.

IV. Whatever your age, have a percentage of your investments in tax-free bonds, fixed income, and cash.

V.   When you invest in the stock market, always use dollar cost averaging. Never put hunks of money in the market at one time.

VI. Pray a lot.

VII. When you invest, invest in index funds or with managers who have low fees and do great research.

VIII. Avoid all hedge funds. Have you noticed that all hedge-fund managers are billionaires?

IX. Buy enough life insurance so that your family is secure should you meet your untimely demise. Every $1 million should yield you a tax-free $40,000 a year. Therefore,

$5 million should produce a tax-free $200,000 a year for your family to live on. Ask yourself if they could they live on that amount comfortably.

X.   If it seems too good to be true, it's too good to be true.

It may seem odd to you that in a book about the business of running a law firm, I would veer into personal financial strategy. However, it has **everything to do with the way you run your business**. I have had dinner with some of American's great trial lawyers, and they are some of the most irresponsible people when it comes to financial matters. I think there is a good reason for it. Like great athletes, and to a certain degree even more so, they believe that the good times will last forever. They believe that even though they take extravagant vacations, overextend their personal credit, and have huge mortgages; they will hit a home run and catch up quickly because of their greatness.

As we all know, the athlete does get old, and the athlete does get injured. Something like 70 percent of all NFL players have filed for personal bankruptcy! Because some trial lawyers suddenly wake up and find themselves fifty years old, they often start taking outsized risks in an effort to be ready for a safe retirement. These outsized risks often lead to financial calamity and potential bankruptcy inside the firm.

By running your personal life in a very cautious and conservative manner, you are empowered to take many more risks in your professional life. There is no profession out there that has the same risks as those of the trial lawyer. We are all risk-takers and gunslingers. That is simply who we are. My bankers are often surprised by the conservative nature of my financial strategy. When they ask me why, the answer is simple. By having a conservative personal financial base, I am able to take risks that, for many, could prove calamitous. The last thing your business needs you to do late in your career is throw Hail Marys and hope that Franco Harris will catch the football off another player's helmet for a touchdown and a Super Bowl victory.

Finally, once you have made the commitment to a conservative personal financial lifestyle, it is then important to build a Black Swan Strategy inside of your own law firm. When the world was crashing at the end of 2008 and we all discovered that we knew nothing, I began to take a very hard look at my law firm and convened emergency sessions to develop what I called the Black Swan Strategy.

For the first time, my partners and I examined potential events we had never, **ever** contemplated. For instance, insurance companies would crash along with the banks. If enough insurance companies file for bankruptcy, there is not enough Black Swan Strategy in the world to save you. The only thing that would save you and your family then would be having your own personal Black Swan Strategy. Once we gathered ourselves, we became convinced that the insurance casualty companies were, for the most part, properly regulated (unlike the banks), but there were risks to some, and some of them would use this season of disaster to pretend there were problems in paradise.

Therefore, as we gathered in our bunker, one of the things that we discussed was, what if X percent of insurance companies failed? What then? The discussions were very unpleasant because it meant our business would be in disarray and we would be hanging on for dear life.

I could spend an entire book discussing what went on in my firm in 2008 as we prepared for our future. Suffice to say, it had us examining firm practices and budgetary items, and it made us, for the first time, put systems into place that would allow us to quickly pull levers that would stop spending and allow us to survive.

I believe it is helpful to all of you to prepare just such a strategy. The exercise goes something like this. What are some of the black swans that could fly into your life? Here are some examples:

1. Insurance companies filing bankruptcy

2. Tort reform

3. Producers leave the firm with no employment contracts or partnership agreements

4. Defense lawyers come to understand you have no trial lawyers in your firm and your weaknesses are exposed

5. Valuable staff members seem to resign at an alarming pace

6. You unexpectedly lose a series of big cases at trial

7. The death of a key man or key woman

8. Your financial institution is acquired or decides not to advance you any further funding

9. The world, the practice of law, and technology is passing you by or has passed you by and you just realized it

These are all black swan events, and any one or more can be lethal. It is important that you as a firm discuss this potential and ask yourselves a very simple question: are we prepared? Do we have a plan? You must establish contingency plans for both bringing in fees and controlling costs. You can spend a whole lot of time at Harvard Business School, but the rule of business is very simple when it comes to making money and having good profits. Take revenue in and control spending. The more money you take in and the better your controls on your spending, the higher the level of profitability in your firm. You do not need to be a Harvard MBA to understand that.

Earlier, we discussed ways to look for new practice areas, geographic areas, and projects to increase firm revenue. When you sit in your planning session—and I recommend it not be an emergency session—I would suggest you spend a lot of time on your budget and making plans for events that could cause the potential and total ruination of your firm.

This session was quite illuminating, and we now have levers and buttons in place that we can pull or push at a moment's notice to save our firm, even if an albatross flies into the jets engines. Again, without spending one hundred pages discussing this, I will just point out a few things.

You need to go down through your costs and budget and look at two categories of items.

1. Items you could absolutely eliminate in a state of emergency with no repercussions.

2. Items you could eliminate or drastically reduce that would result in repercussions that would be acceptable given that without these repercussions, you may not have a firm tomorrow.

The most obvious things in the first category are such line items as Christmas parties, travel and seminars, cell phones, club memberships, and on and on it goes. You get the picture. There is then a second tier of line items that, while painful in to eliminate, may be the only thing that stands between you and shutting your doors. Elimination or drastic cutbacks of 401(k) and firm contributions, salary freezes, and replacing personnel that should have gone a long time ago with personnel who are more vibrant and less expensive, etc. Finally, you will find that the two above tranches give the firm some relief and then there are extreme measures. They are extreme to the point that you worry you will lose lawyers and personnel, but without acting, you may lose your firm: salary reductions, increased healthcare participation by employees, reduction or suspension of advertising, elimination of partner draws altogether, elimination of practice areas that are extremely risky or maybe not even profitable.

Again, because of the complexity of this subject, I am only giving you discussion points and ideas. The central thought here is this: plan for the day the tsunami approaches. Have devices in place that can sense the tsunami miles off the coast and don't be caught running for high ground when the black cloud is over your cabana. By having an emergency plan in place now, you will be able to act rationally later.

BLACK SWAN CONTINGENCY CONSIDERATION

Here are very simple things you can do now to prepare your firm for the potential day when a black swan flies in.

1. Pay cash for equipment.

2. Borrow as little of client costs as possible.

3. Examine the cost of rent or mortgage on your office.

4. Bid office supplies on a yearly basis (three separate bids).

5. Bid **all** insurance on a yearly basis. Remember, friends in the insurance business can be expensive.

6. Closely examine your costs for health insurance, and spend a great deal of time talking about co-pay by employees.

7. Examine your salary structure to determine if it is higher than your competitors'.

8. Take a close look at your advertising budget and make sure you are receiving the most bang for your buck. I cannot begin to tell you how many clients we now represent at Practice Made Perfect who were paying five, six, and seven times too much for their advertising.

9. Don't let the deadwood build up; it can sink the ship.

10. Discuss the benefits and perks your staff and attorneys are receiving.

11. This one will be difficult. Have a very heart-to-heart discussion on compensation and partnership-sharing by those at the highest level.

12. Resolve to implement as many of the suggestions laid out in this book as possible. Running your law practice like a business is the key.

I know that this chapter has lasted longer than the others, and there is a reason for that. It is because the unknown is what usually takes us down. When we discuss how firms come and go in a later chapter, the most common refrain is, "We never saw it coming." The best rule of thumb I have found is to **always** assume that it is coming. Always hope for the best, but be prepared for the worst. The way that you conduct your personal life financially will have a direct bearing on the success of your business life. Far too often, successful and skilled trial lawyers don't seem to understand that this dichotomy is really one in the same. Being conservative in your personal life allows you to be much bolder in your business life. It is not what you know that matters; it is what you don't know.

Have a plan! Be prepared! Black swans are just around the corner!

"We don't know what we don't know."

—Scott W. Weinstein

14

STAYING NUMBER ONE

It's Not Good in Englewood

Years ago, Shaquille O'Neal and Kobe Bryant led the Los Angeles Lakers to repeated national championships. It seemed that there was almost nothing that could stop them for nearly a decade. Then, suddenly, egos became outsized, Shaq was gone, and Kobe remained as the leader of a shattered team. The next season was a disaster, and the Lakers became a cream puff. The Lakers' practice facility is located in Englewood, California. It was not good in Englewood. All of a sudden, the once-mighty Lakers had a point guard named Smush. Charles Barkley commented that nobody was going to be a champion with a point guard named Smush.

If you were a young lawyer in the seventies, your portfolio had Fortune 500 stocks that it seemed would be the bedrock of your future retirement strategy. Eastern Airlines. Kmart. Sears. Enron. The list goes on and on. Companies that were great and built to last—companies it seemed would go on and on forever. Becoming number one is one thing—staying number one is another.

In studying great firms and great companies that have collapsed, I have seen a common thread that defines them all. One or more of the following factors always seem to be in play.

Ego

The outsized ego is perhaps more dangerous to your firm than any other factor. The great trial lawyer usually has an overinflated ego to begin with, but when you put her inside a law firm, she can sometimes become unbearable.

Young lawyers who start with a firm later develop into real forces of their own, yet the leader always sees those lawyers as associates or fledgling wannabes. Failing to recognize the true superstars of your firm and not allowing them to sit at the table as full partners causes more splits than you can imagine. The young lawyer is now forty years old, and the old bull may be in his sixties. The old bull often refuses because his ego won't let him or he truly doesn't see the forest through the trees.

The old bull refuses to recognize that in looking at his young partner, he is actually looking at himself twenty-some odd years ago. Whether it's stubbornness, an unwillingness to let go, or an inability to see the truth, frictions exist, and before you know it, the young partner and a group of young bulls are planning and preparing for their coup d'état. The result is predictable: lawsuits, bar grievances, severed friendships and relationships, and families who used to vacation together refusing to acknowledge each other in the elevator.

To stay number one, it is important that leaders recognize that time moves on and new superstars emerge. There was Larry Bird before Michael Jordan and Michael Jordan before LeBron James. As time marches on, so do dynamics. The firm that fails to realize these dynamics may never become number one, and if they have been number one, they will soon find they are not even play-off worthy.

Greed

Federal prisons in the United States are littered with the former CEOs of Fortune 500 companies, and, unfortunately, some of

America's great trial lawyers. Greed has been with us since the beginning of time. It is a character trait that proves to be predictably fatal. For many, there is never such a thing as enough. One of the greatest trial lawyers and richest men in America sits locked up in prison because enough wasn't enough.

Firms shatter into smithereens because of greed. When I visit with a lawyer—whether it be an old bull or a young Turk—in the postmortem of a split-up, I get to hear his side of the story. Invariably, when we finally boil down all the issues and synthesize the facts, they broke up over peanuts.

You sit there scratching your head and saying to yourself, "You broke up this well-oiled machine that produced at a high level, and now the whole is nowhere near as great as what the sum of its parts once was." It is important when dealing with such matters to sit back and put things into perspective. As the old saying goes, many times people will cut off their noses to spite their faces. Their greed and egos simply won't let them cede a few dollars when those few dollars would multiply for them for the rest of their lives. Too many firms live in a feast-or-famine environment.

I have found the ones that do not are the ones that have very fair sharing arrangements. There are no peaks and valleys in these firms—only lush green fields. When you face these problems as you begin your journey to number one or in your quest to stay number one, remember that perspective is everything.

The Cancer Cell

The cancer cell is one of the most insidious and dangerous plagues that can fall onto a firm. The cancer cell can be one or two people—a high-ranking staff member of the management team or support staff, or one of the lawyers inside the firm. Either way, this cancer begins as a small cell and, unless eradicated, can spread to infect the entire firm.

Once upon a time, I had a lawyer who was a cancer cell inside of my law firm. One of the dangers of the cancer is that many times, you don't know it's there until it's too late. Cancer can be the silent killer. The cancer inside a firm is usually there because you have allowed it to exist and decided to do nothing.

My own story involves a lawyer who I thought the world of and actually treated in a special way. We are talking about someone of very average talent who was making seven figures plus on a regular basis. As much as I cared for and had done for this individual, I would still hear through the grapevine of the carping, sniping, and undermining that was going on behind my back. For whatever reason, I chose to remain silent and, for the longest time, did nothing. This lawyer would move throughout the firm, go inside offices, close doors, and rip the fabric of the firm apart. Even though he was making serious money and had been treated more than fairly based upon his capabilities, the incessant backstabbing continued.

I have yet to understand how well-compensated cancer cells decide to begin their campaign of destruction, but I can tell you that the longer they remain untreated, the more likely it is that the cells will grow throughout the firm until the tumor is inoperable.

Once our cancer cell had left the firm, the damage he had done was palpable. The lawyers he had infected had an edge and a grudge for no real reason. It wasn't until I fully understood what had to be done that I began to eradicate the remaining effects of the cancer. I fired lawyers. They were shocked. Some asked for reconsideration, and I granted it. Some I fired and never let back in. For those who were allowed to stay after being fired and asking for reconsideration, I explained to them in no uncertain terms that, in the future, I would not tolerate the behavior and conduct of the past. The lawyers who were fired and not allowed to return provided a strong message to everyone else that the days of closed-door backstabbing and destabilization were over.

The same thing can happen with non-lawyer staff. A cancer cell is usually someone whom one partner has a very strong allegiance to yet the rest of the firm detests. That non-lawyer cancer can be as destabilizing as the other form of cancer, the lawyer cancer. The non-lawyer cancer goes throughout the firm causing trouble and wreaking mayhem. He has the propensity to make trouble for trouble's sake. He is looking for power just for power's sake. In my early years, I turned a blind eye to the cancer cells in my firm. As the lyrics to the Rod Stewart song go, "I wish that I knew what I know now when I was younger." Had I the foresight, I would have summarily fired the lawyer cancer three years before he finally left. I would have fired the insensitive and conniving HR manager one day after I really knew what should be done.

I cannot overemphasize the importance of examining these diseases that soak into the flesh of your firm and begin to eat it alive through a clear lens. The danger is that people begin to buy into their negativity, and, before you know it, your whole firm is a corrosive environment.

The rule of thumb that I will leave you with is simple: if a person doesn't want to be in your law firm, you don't want that person in your law firm. While there may have been a time that you had great affection for them or they have some talents that are beneficial to the firm, you can't eradicate cancer without surgery, chemotherapy, and radiation.

Cancer kills!

They Never Saw It Coming

This is the most dangerous problem that a firm can face. Whether it be because those in the firm are aging and can't get out of their own way or because they want to run with blinders on their whole lives, they just never saw it coming.

Kmart never saw Walmart, and let this be a Nostradamus prediction: Walmart never saw Amazon. Now, Walmart, the greatest retailer in the history of the world, is scrambling to develop an "Amazon solution." Just because you are great doesn't mean you always will be great.

If it's not broke, break it!

There are warning signs all around us that should allow us to know what is coming. The superstar young associate or partner. Certain areas of tort reform. Competitors that surge while you turn a blind eye. Technology both inside and outside your office and as a way of generating new business. The potential threats are countless but should be counted.

When the ostrich sticks her head in the sand, she does so because she thinks that if she can't see you, you can't see her. Thank God we don't hunt ostriches. They would surely be extinct. The law firm graveyards across America are littered with ostriches. In the law firm business, the ostrich is a hunted bird.

Have you ever heard that a person is playing possum? We all think that means that a person is playing like he is either asleep or dead in the hopes that he will be left alone. I am sure that in the years of war in the world, many soldiers have played possum on battlefields. I am sure they have survived because the opposing soldiers thought they were dead, took their weapons, and moved on. Many law firms in America play possum every day. They hope that by laying motionless on the ground, they will not be disturbed and can get up and go about their business.

I would like to let you in on a little secret that has greatly changed the way I do business. Science tells us that when a possum is in a trance-like state, they are not simply trying to fool us. They are, in fact, paralyzed in a rigid state induced by sheer, unadulterated fear. That's right. They are scared shitless! There are firms in your cities that are playing possum as we speak. At the end of the day, as collegial as we all want to be, we want each other's business. It is not a personal thing—just reality. It is no more personal than Toyota wanting to sell a car to someone who is thinking about buying a Honda. Nothing evil. Nothing bad. Just the facts. In our business world of law, the firm that decides to play possum and to hide like an ostrich is doomed to failure. Being number one and staying number one will take all of your best-kept attributes, energy, and drive. It is not impossible, as we know from firms we respect throughout America. Baron & Budd. Levin, Papantonio. Weitz & Luxenberg. Those great firms have survived and sustained for decades while others form elephant graveyards throughout America.

At the end of the day, Kobe Bryant and the Lakers realized that Kobe Bryant could not do it alone. Phil Jackson, the Hall of Fame coach, was no more effective at coaching Kobe and Smush than I would have been. Fortunately, in sports, a rich owner can remedy a situation and pay big dollars to bring in superstars. In the practice of law, when a firm is incinerated, it **never** rises from the ashes. There are no second chances. Jerry Buss and the Lakers finally realized the error of their ways. Kobe had to realize that without other great players, he was incapable of winning a championship. The Lakers locked and reloaded. Out was Smush and in was Lamar Odom and Pau Gasol. With this strong supporting cast, Kobe Bryant was not triple-teamed, but instead left alone to score, assist, and rebound. They went from an eighth-place team in the West to the National Champions in 2009. Ego. Greed. Inability to reflect inwardly. The internal cancer cell. All of these factors destroy great companies and great law firms. Remember, it is truly good to be great, but you cannot be great without a great team around you. Johnny Cochran used to say that there is no "I" in team. Yes, it is an overused cliché, but maybe there is a reason that it is overused. **Because it is the truth.**

15

SAM WALTON

Swim Upstream

For the last one hundred some odd pages, I have inundated you with my pearls of wisdom, life experiences, business strategies, thoughts on the future, and thoughts about the past. A few may have already known most, or some, of what I said. However, confirmation is always healthy. Hopefully, most of you have picked up pearls and gems along the way that will help you build great law firms.

My last words of wisdom, however, are the most important. After all you have read and all that you know, there is still one impediment that is so powerful that even with the knowledge you have and the rational thinking you possess, you will still be incapable of pulling the trigger. It is not a thing but an emotion.

Fear.

Franklin Roosevelt addressed our country at its greatest time of peril, and his words, if you will excuse the language, still live with us in infamy. "We have nothing to fear, but fear itself." Fear is a paralyzing emotion. The great gunslingers in the Wild West had no fear. Wyatt Earp would simply step out onto a dusty road and say, "Draw." Trial lawyer John O'Quinn of Texas understood that feeling of exhilaration, as do countless other trial lawyers throughout America. They know and believe that they will win because of their sheer force of will. Ice water courses through their veins, and there is not one drop of fear in their bodies. Fear makes cowards of us all. The great lawyers and businesspeople do not possess that emotion. Years ago in Arkansas, a five-and-dime operator by the name of Sam Walton had a vision. He believed that his Ben Franklin store nestled on Main Street was a dinosaur in waiting. He knew that if he were to avoid the fate of the dinosaur, he had to move boldly and without fear. At the same time, he had a second vision: to offer shoppers items at a deep, deep discount, without frills. He believed that price would trump personality.

Walton closed that store and built a stand-alone building that became the first beachhead for what is Walmart today. Woolworths, Ben Franklin stores, all of them—they never saw it coming. Their blinders were affixed to the sides of their heads. Their egos and raw greed did not allow them to change course or spend money in a new way. And then, in a blink of an eye, they were all gone.

I have studied Sam Walton and his ways my whole life. Walton was a visionary and a pioneer. His methodology and business habits play right into the hands of the successful law firm. Walton didn't believe in frills. He flew an old, beat-up plane. When he went out of town on business, he would stay at a budget hotel and share a room with one of his managers. He drove around town in a red pickup truck. He had a vision and a purpose. He had a winning business with the Ben Franklin stores, and he decided to break it into a thousand pieces. I suggest you purchase *The 10 Rules of Sam Walton: Success Secrets for Remarkable Results.* He tells us in this book that all of the rules are important, but one of the rules is greater than the other nine put together.

Swim upstream.

In business and in law, everybody is in the same stream. For the most part, they are all traveling the same way—with the current! They are perched on top of inner tubes and coated in sunscreen with lip balm applied, a frosty margarita affixed to their right hand, and a big black cigar attached to their left. They are all moving at about the same speed because they are all riding the current. Some may be going a little faster because they actually get off their float and kick for periods of time. Some have even taken the bold step of putting a small motor on the back of their dinghy, and they are the leaders of the pack. But for only a minute.

As all of these businesses float and putter, Walton is there with no float and no water wings, swimming upstream. His head is down. He kicks rhythmically. His stroke is precise. His goggles allow him to see the river bottom clearly, and he swims against the current. He swims upstream.

As all of the river rats breeze past him, they look and they laugh. What a fool.

However, Walton teaches us all a lesson that should never be forgotten. The current that takes these people down the river leads them to places they may not know exist. For all they know, they may be on a river that is attached to Niagara Falls, and even a wooden barrel won't help them in the end. What Walton teaches us is that when you swim upstream, there is certainty. At the top of a river is high and dry land. Usually, the soil is very fertile and rich for planting a bountiful harvest. To swim upstream, you must have no fear. You must have endurance. You must live by the motto, "Nothing is about today; everything is about tomorrow." You must believe in yourself, and you must have a work ethic that is equal to none. You also must strip off your blinders of the past and put on a pair of binoculars that allow you to see the future in 360 degrees.

As we took this journey together, I gave you my best thoughts about your future. Even as I conclude this chapter on a sunny day on the beach in Ponce Inlet, Florida, I am scared to death about my firm's future. There is a difference, though, between being scared and being fearful. Being scared is normal. It allows your adrenaline to run and for you to work without an alarm clock or self-imposed deadlines. Our race is a marathon—not a sprint, and I wish each one of you the greatest success as you attempt to become number one, stay number one, and become a sustainable, multimillion-dollar law firm.

Happy fishing!

Swim upstream!